Table of Contents

Forward — iii

Introduction — v

Chapter 1. The Record-breaking Winter of 2009-10 — 1

Chapter 2. Washingtons Top 10 Snowstorms — 11

Chapter 3. Historic Snowstorms - A Photo Comparison with Snowmageddon — 25

Chapter 4. The December 5 Coincidence — 37

Chapter 5. Snowpocalypse - The Blizzard of December 18-19, 2009 — 45

Chapter 6. The Alberta Clipper of January 8, 2010 — 59

Chapter 7. The Snowstorm of January 30, 2010 — 67

Chapter 8. Snowmageddon's Appetizer - February 2-3, 2010 — 73

Chapter 9. Snowmageddon - The Blizzard of February 5-6, 2010 — 79

Chapter 10. Snoverkill - The Blizzard of February 9-10, 2010 — 97

Acknowledgments — 112

Bibliography — 113

Cars buried in snow near Cleveland Park.
February 10, 2010
Ian Livingston

Sunrise on the Mall
February 15, 2010
Kevin Ambrose

Foreward

I am so thrilled to have lived in Washington D.C. during what will one day be known as the legendary winter of 2009-10. As a well-known winter weather enthusiast, author of *Northeast Snowstorms* and the former Winter Weather Expert for the Weather Channel, I never thought I would experience such a winter in the Washington area in my lifetime and I've spent many winters here.

For much of the metropolitan Washington area, this was the snowiest winter on record, with records dating back to the 1880s. The greatest December snowstorm on record on December 18-19 made for a very White Christmas. If that wasn't enough to produce a memorable winter in a region where big snowstorms can occur, but often not for many years at a time, the greatest back-to-back punch of extreme snowstorms occurred later on February 5-6 and 9-10 . These two storms overwhelmed and shut down the region for many days, felled numerous trees and tree limbs, left hundreds of thousands without power and left a state of emergency in which even emergency vehicles and personnel were prohibited from being outside.

While the winter will long be remembered for the inconveniences suffered by many Washington residents, the winter of 2009-10 will also provide lasting memories for a lifetime, especially for the children, snow lovers, and the many interested in how nature at its extreme can turn familiar surroundings into magical places.

This book describes the winter of 2009-10, accompanied by many photos that will capture the spirit and beauty of the winter in the Nation's Capital. The photos also show winter weather conditions that have never been quite so extreme in the area.

Paul Kocin
NOAA Meteorologist

The Mall during Snowmageddon
February 6, 2010
Ian Livingston

Snowmageddon Snow Cover
February 7, 2010
NASA's Terra Satellite

Introduction

As a meteorologist, the *Washington Post's* weather editor, and snow enthusiast, I never imagined the D.C. area would experience snows like those of the winter 2009-10. I always considered the snow record set in 1898-99 as untouchable, especially as our region's snowfall averages were declining in previous decades.

But as the Snoverkill blizzard raged into the afternoon of February 10, the winter of 2009-10 established itself as the snowfall king, and with authority. The heavy snow, 30-40 mph winds, and plunging temperatures produced the most extreme whiteout conditions I have ever witnessed in the Washington area. As the flakes finally tapered off that evening and I stepped into the chest-high snow, drifting above the roofs of cars, I realized I was part of a scene I may never experience again. The eerily quiet, transformed landscape felt like a foreign place, more closely resembling ski country or some land well to the north. As a snow lover, it was awe-inspiring.

The season featured two top ten snowstorms in D.C. (three in Baltimore), Dulles Airport exceeding 30" in a single snow event, and all three area airports setting seasonal snowfall records! Snow cover exceeded an incredible 40 inches in many spots after the Snoverkill blizzard. It was truly a remarkable winter. Although it was delightful for many of us snow lovers throughout the area, the crippling storms caused major disruptions ranging from power outages to business, government, and school closures, to car accidents.

This book will step you through each snow event of the winter of 2009-10, accompanied by surface weather maps, radar images, weather analysis, and plenty of snowy photographs. Many of the photographs in the book were taken by the authors, Kevin Ambrose and Ian Livingston, while others were taken by area photographers. The photos show our beautiful Washington landmarks and suburban areas, all buried by a historic blanket of snow.

You can relive Snowmageddon and the amazing winter of 2009-10 every time you open this book. It may even bring back some fun and/or challenging memories. Think snow!

> Jason Samenow
> Weather Editor
> *The Washington Post*

Measuring new snow in Oakton, VA.
February 6, 2010
Kevin Ambrose

The Marine Corps Memorial in snow.
February 7, 2010
The United States Park Police

Chapter 1.

The Record-breaking Winter of 2009-10

The National Mall.
February 12, 2010
Kevin Ambrose

Washington recorded a record-breaking 56.1" of snow during the 2009-10 winter season.

The Record-breaking Winter of 2009-10

The 2009-10 winter season was highlighted by historic snowfalls in late December and early February, breaking all-time records for monthly and seasonal totals. The federal government was closed for almost a week during the winter and both Virginia and Maryland declared states of emergency on multiple occasions. In February, it took more than a week before some residents were finally dug out from the snow. Large earthmovers were used when snow plows were unable to clear the snow from residential streets. Washington even received more snow than cities in New England.

Location	2009-10 Snow Total	Season Average
Washington	56.1"	15.2"
Dulles	73.2"	21.2"
Baltimore	77.0"	18.2"

Sunrise on the Mall.
February 15, 2010

Kevin Ambrose

Great Falls in snow.
February 7, 2010

The United States Park Police

As of 2010, Washington receives 15.2" of snow during an average winter season. Looking back in the record books, the Washington area receives a 10" snowstorm about every five years and a historic snowstorm of 15" or greater roughly every 10-15 years.

Put three historic snowstorms into a single winter season and you get the amazing and historic winter of 2009-10. Seasonal snowfall records were broken at all three area airports and Dulles Airport set an amazing single snowstorm record of 32.4" for the February 5-6 Snowmageddon storm.

The winter of 2009-10 began with an early-season snowstorm on December 5, with up to 7" of snow accumulating across the area. Later in the month, a snowstorm on December 18-19 broke all December snowstorm records for the area, with totals of 16" to 26".

January began quiet, with a weak Alberta Clipper storm system dropping an inch of snow on January 8. In late January the storm track turned active. From January 30 to February 10, four snowstorms dropped up to 60" of snow across the region. The largest storms in February occurred on February 5-6 and February 9-10. The February 5-6 storm was heaviest in the western and northern suburbs and the February 9-10 storm was heaviest in the northern suburbs. Washington's final seasonal snowfall total of 56.1" broke the record of 54.4" set during the winter of 1898-99.

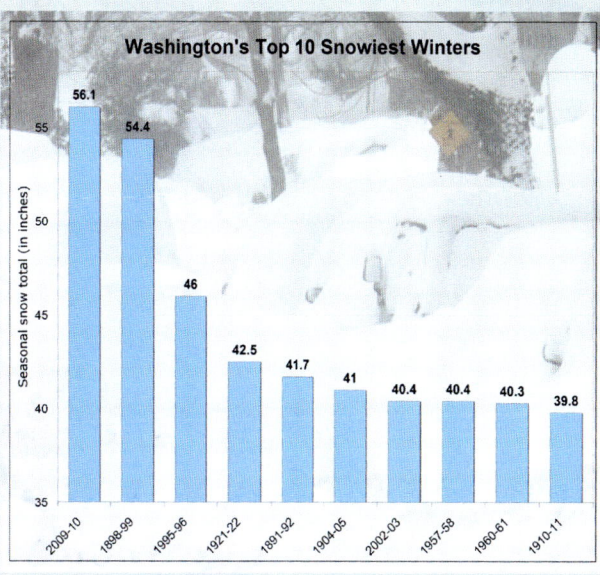

Washington's top 10 snowiest winters (above) and the top 10 snowiest winters for Dulles Airport and Baltimore (below).

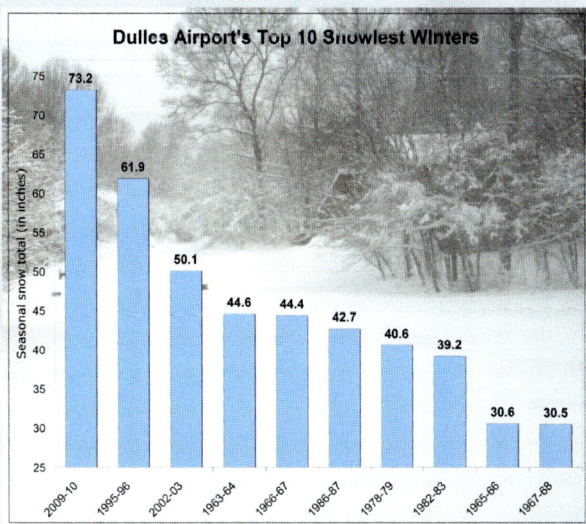

Seasonal Snowfall - Winter of 2009-10

Snowfall Total in Inches
- < 15
- 15 - 30
- 31 - 45
- 46 - 60
- 61 - 75
- 76 - 90
- 91 - 105

Map by Katie Wheatley

The Drivers of 2009-10's Historic Snowfall

Weather is an intricate mix of multiple variables, and in winter around D.C. the mix often fails to materialize as much as snow lovers wish. In 2009-10, the story was different. While no individual storm can be wholly attributed to any one climate variable, there is little doubt that two main factors contributed to Washington's snowiest winter on record.

These two factors are known as the El Nino Southern Oscillation (ENSO) and the North Atlantic Oscillation (NAO). For simplicity in the summaries in later pages of this book, the NAO is referred to as the "Greenland Block."

El Nino is characterized by warming of the equatorial Pacific. The warming shifts airflow patterns and creates an energetic southern jet stream. El Nino's prevailing storm track historically brings more activity, and thus increased rainfall, to the southern United States as far north as the mid-Atlantic. El Nino also often brings cooler than normal conditions to the southeast U.S., thanks in large to increased storminess.

Before winter began, the Pacific was well into an El Nino phase of ENSO (as opposed to La Nina or neutral conditions). Forecasters, such as those at the *Washington Post's* Capital Weather Gang, saw this as a clear signal that the mid-Atlantic was at higher than usual risk for an active southern storm track and moisture-laden storms.

As its name suggests, the NAO refers to a pattern presiding over the northern Atlantic Ocean. Unlike El Nino, the NAO is wholly atmospheric in nature, and is characterized by air pressure differences over the high latitudes. Winter to winter, the NAO is the dominant feature of climate variability in the Eastern U.S. and into Europe.

A positive NAO often brings warmth to the East Coast along with fast-moving storms, as a strong low pressure near Iceland keeps systems progressing east. During a negative NAO, higher pressure in the north helps send colder air south. Storms occurring in a negative NAO regime may become more ferocious near the East Coast and produce snowier conditions. This is thanks to enhanced cold sources and a more amplified (or steep south to north) jet stream over the region.

The feature most commonly associated with a negative NAO is referred to as a Greenland Block because the high pressure in question centers itself over or very near that island. A Greenland Block helps lock cold air in place over the East Coast whereas, in its absence, the necessary cold air for snow often erodes and/or moves off into the Atlantic Ocean. The block also tends to generate a storm system log jam, resulting in longer lasting storms with the potential to produce more snow.

A Greenland Block is favorable for, but not a guarantee of, a snowstorm in the region. Many of Washington's, and the East Coast as a whole, biggest snowstorms come during negative NAO phases that feature blocking. Studies such as those in Paul Kocin and Louis Uccellini's *Northeast Snowstorms Volume 1* have found that roughly 2/3 of major snowstorms on the East Coast occurred during a negative phase of the NAO. Positive phase storms accounted for only about 1/6 of cases.

This Oakton, VA neighborhood shoveled a gathering place to share food and drink and to discuss the snowy predicament of being snowbound for a week due to unplowed roads. The atmosphere was always festive, complete with a illuminated palm tree.

Kevin Ambrose

Comparing the Winters of 1898-99 and 2009-10

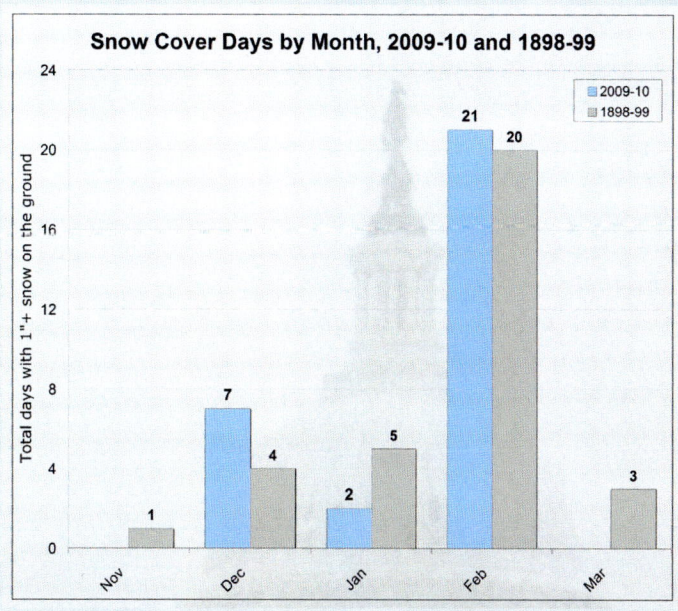

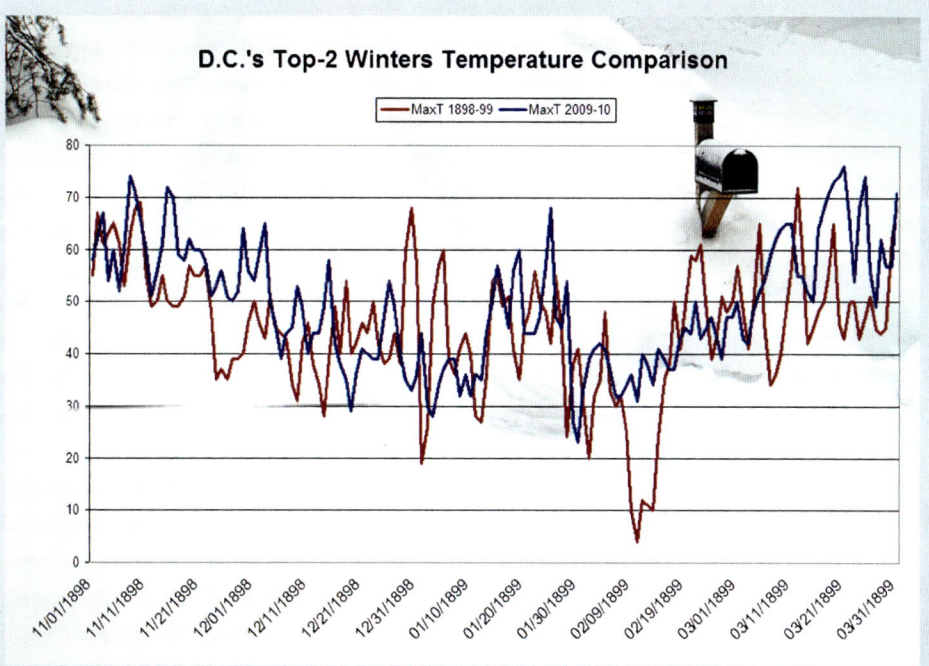

For over a century, the winter of 1898-99 held Washington's seasonal snowfall record at 54.9". The closest runner-up to this record was the winter of 1995-96, at 46". Then, on December 5, 2009, the first snowstorm of the season occurred. By the end of the winter, 56.1" of snow had fallen, breaking the snowfall record of 1898-99 by over an inch. The charts above compare the two winters by high temperature and snow cover days to get a deeper understanding of how the winters compared to one another.

The Knickerbocker Snowstorm, January 27-28, 1922.
Washington, D.C.
The Library of Congress

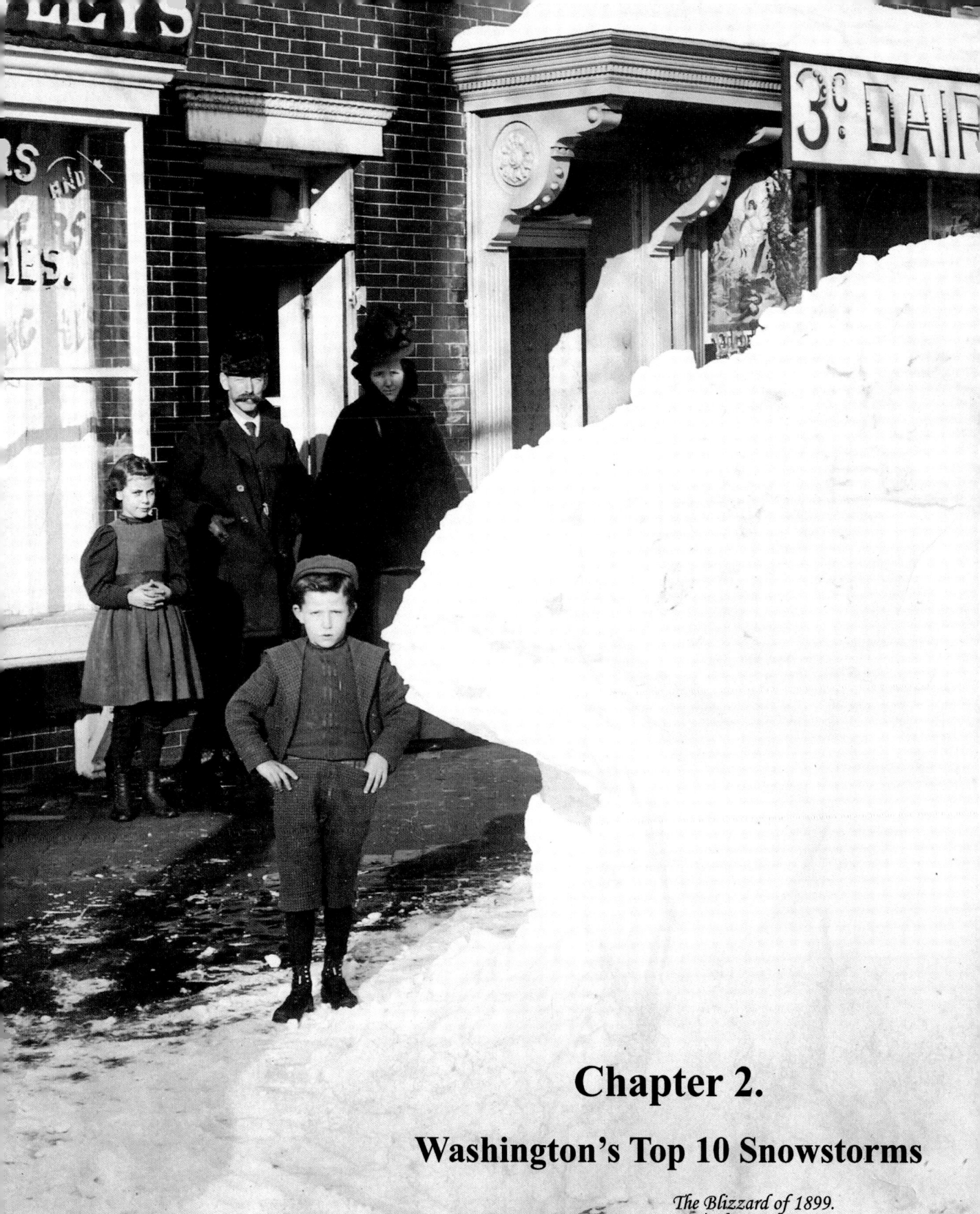

Chapter 2.
Washington's Top 10 Snowstorms

*The Blizzard of 1899.
Washington, D.C.
Library of Congress*

Washington's Top 10 Snowstorms

Washington has a unique winter climate in that the city rarely receives large snowfalls, but when it does, it can compete with, and surpass, many northern cities for quantity of snow within a single storm. We have seen major snow dumps in Washington over the past few decades, including 1983, 1996, 2003, 2009, and 2010.

Of all the big Washington snowstorms, the Knickerbocker Snowstorm of 1922 has set the bar. At 28" of snow, the Knickerbocker will be hard to beat. Several snowstorms have surpassed the Knickerbocker's snow total at locations within the Washington area, but not at the official recording station for D.C.

The Winter of 2009-10 produced two top 10 snowstorms in Washington in one season, an unprecedented occurrance in modern times. A photo and statistical summary of the top 10 snowstorms are included on the pages that follow.

Where to begin? -- February 6, 2010
Washington, D.C.

Ian Livingston

January 28, 1922
Washington, D.C.
Library of Congress

#1 Washington Snowstorm

The Knickerbocker Snowstorm -- January 27-28, 1922

D.C. Snow	28"
Area Snowfall Range	20-32"
D.C. Liquid	2.81"
Temperature Range	18-31 °F
Resulting Snow Cover	15 days
Season Total	42.5"

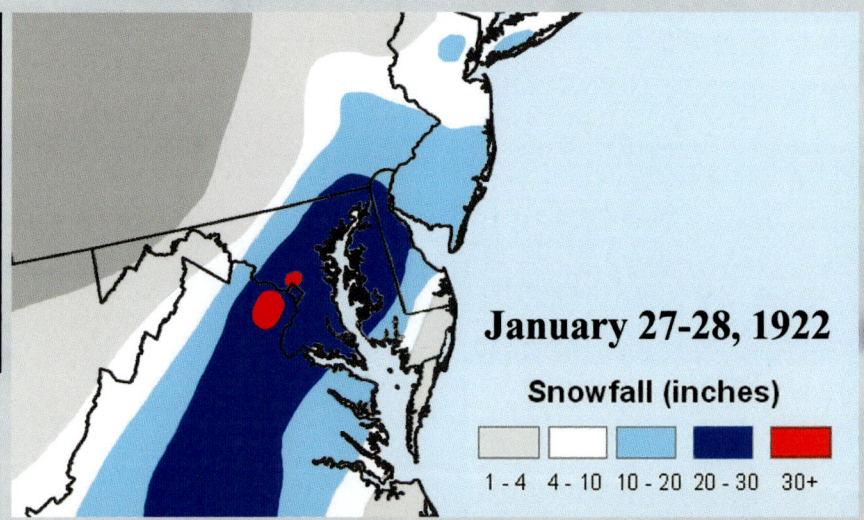

January 27-28, 1922

Snowfall (inches)

1 - 4   4 - 10   10 - 20   20 - 30   30+

February 14, 1899
Washington, D.C.
The Historical Society of Washington

#2 Washington Snowstorm
The Blizzard of February 11-13, 1899

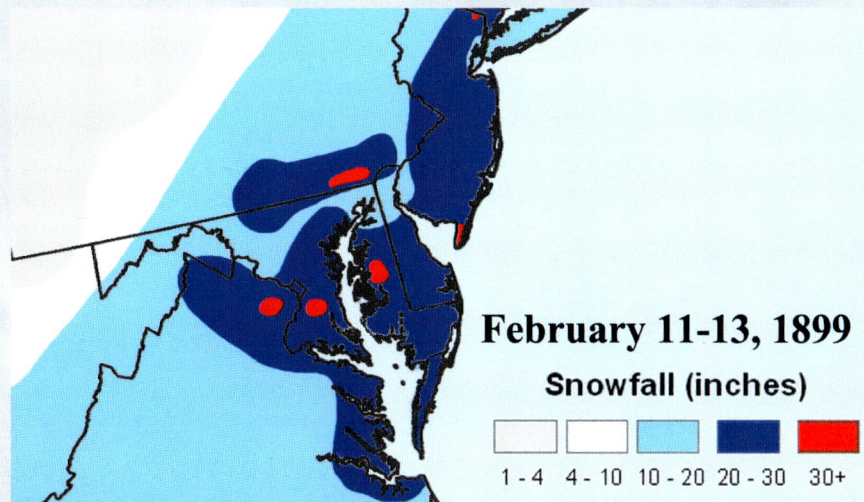

February 11-13, 1899
Snowfall (inches)
1-4 4-10 10-20 20-30 30+

D.C. Snow	20.5"
Area Snowfall Range	18-32"
D.C. Liquid	2.08"
Temperature Range	-15-12 °F
Resulting Snow Cover	11 days
Season Total	54.4"

February 19, 1979
Washington, D.C.

Copyright Washington Post;
Reprinted with permission of the D.C. Public Library

#3 Washington Snowstorm

Presidents' Day Snowstorm -- February 18-19, 1979

D.C. Snow	18.7"
Area Snowfall Range	14-27"
D.C. Liquid	1.37"
Temperature Range	6-36 °F
Resulting Snow Cover	8 days
Season Total	37.7"

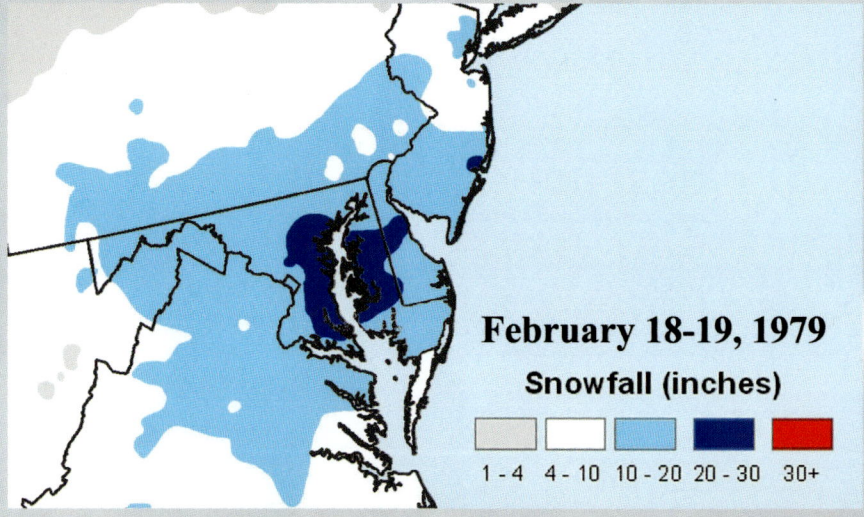

February 18-19, 1979
Snowfall (inches)

1-4 4-10 10-20 20-30 30+

February 6, 2010
Washington, D.C.
Ian Livingston

#4 Washington Snowstorm
Snowmageddon -- February 5-6, 2010

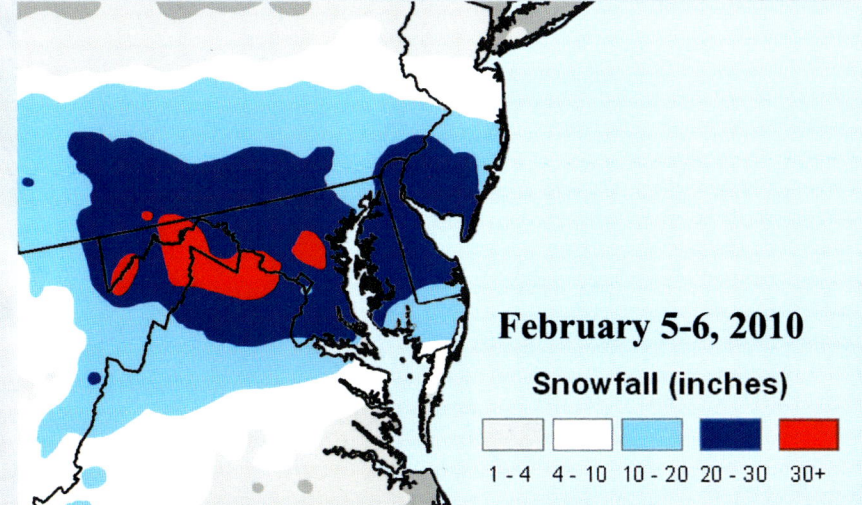

February 5-6, 2010
Snowfall (inches)
1-4   4-10   10-20   20-30   30+

D.C. Snow	17.8"
Area Snowfall Range	17-34"
D.C. Liquid	1.5"
Temperature Range	21-37 °F
Resulting Snow Cover	18 days
Season Total	56.1"

January 7, 1996
The Capitol
AP Photo/Cameron Craig

#5 Washington Snowstorm
The Blizzard of January 6-8, 1996

D.C. Snow	17.1"
Area Snowfall Range	17-31"
D.C. Liquid	1.46"
Temperature Range	18-30 °F
Resulting Snow Cover	13 days
Season Total	46"

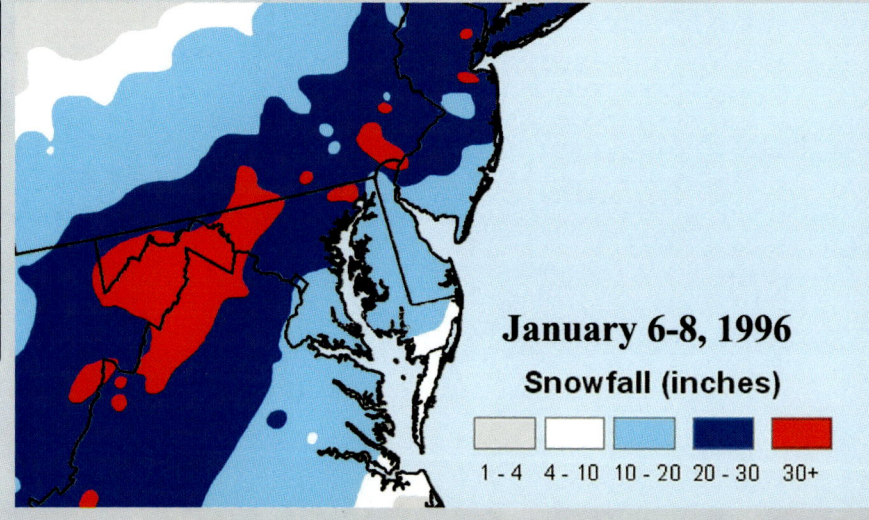

January 6-8, 1996
Snowfall (inches)

1 - 4   4 - 10   10 - 20   20 - 30   30+

February 19, 2003
The Smithsonian
Kevin Ambrose

#6 Washington Snowstorm

Presidents' Day Snowstorm II -- February 16-18, 2003

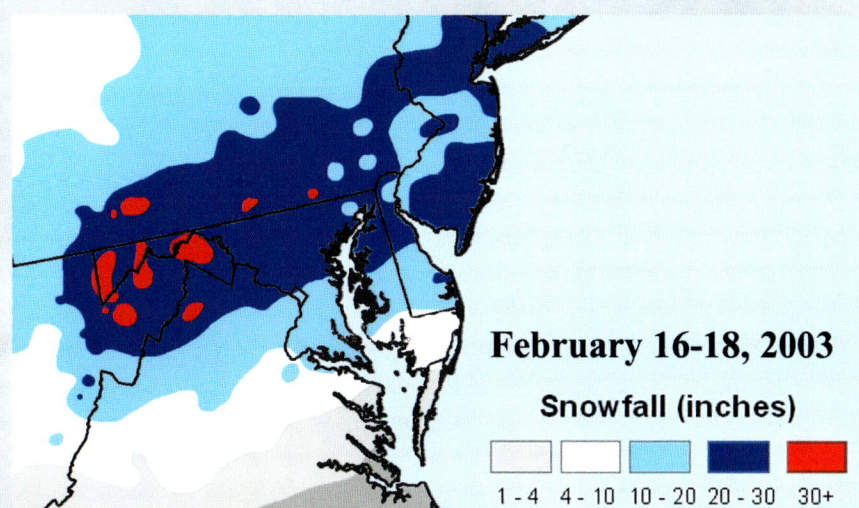

February 16-18, 2003

Snowfall (inches)

1 - 4   4 - 10   10 - 20   20 - 30   30+

D.C. Snow	16.7"
Area Snowfall Range	15-28"
D.C. Liquid	1.58"
Temperature Range	15-35 °F
Resulting Snow Cover	9 days
Season Total	40.4"

February 13, 1983
Frederick, MD

Copyright Washington Post;
Reprinted with permission of the D.C. Public Library

#7 Washington Snowstorm
The Blizzard of February 11-12, 1983

D.C. Snow	16.6"
Area Snowfall Range	16-30"
D.C. Liquid	1.94"
Temperature Range	19-35 °F
Resulting Snow Cover	8 days
Season Total	27.6"

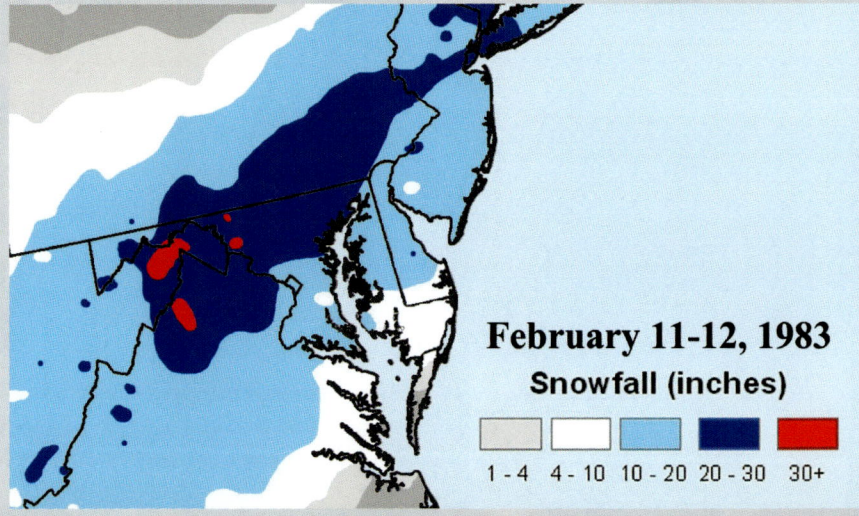

February 11-12, 1983
Snowfall (inches)

1 - 4   4 - 10   10 - 20   20 - 30   30+

December 19, 2009
Washington, D.C.
Ian Livingston

#8 Washington Snowstorm

Snowpocalypse -- December 18-19, 2009

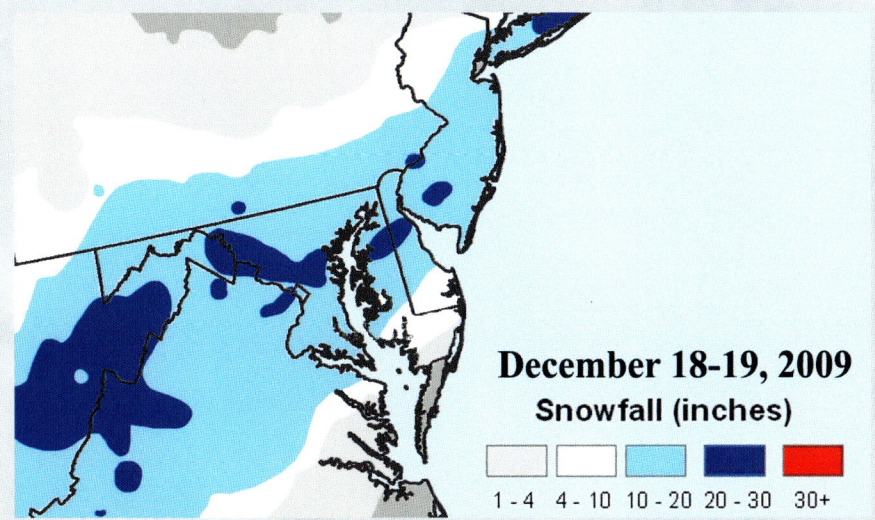

December 18-19, 2009
Snowfall (inches)
1 - 4   4 - 10   10 - 20   20 - 30   30+

D.C. Snow	16.4"
Area Snowfall Range	16-23"
D.C. Liquid	1.45"
Temperature Range	25-35 °F
Resulting Snow Cover	7 days
Season Total	56.1"

February 7, 1936
Washington, D.C.

Copyright Washington Post;
Reprinted with permission of the D.C. Public Library

#9 Washington Snowstorm
The Blizzard of February 7, 1936

D.C. Snow	14.4"
Area Snowfall Range	6-18"
D.C. Liquid	1.01"
Temperature Range	16-25 °F
Resulting Snow Cover	10 days
Season Total	31.8"

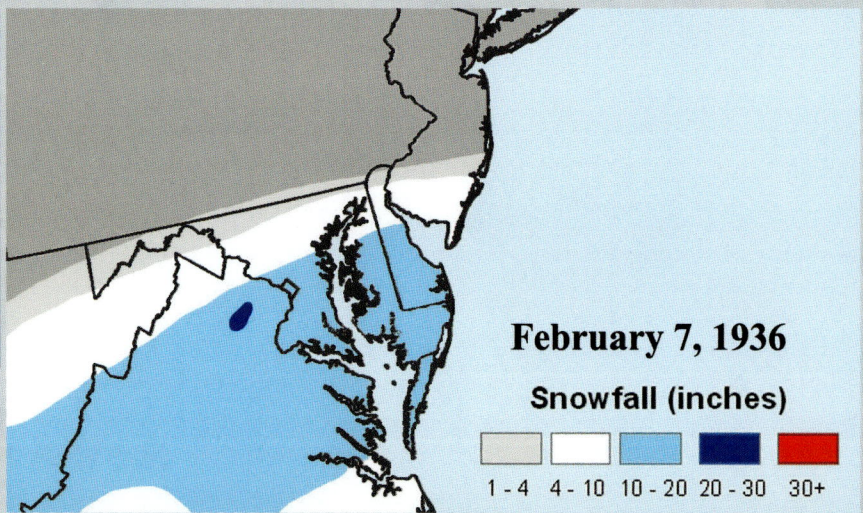

February 7, 1936

Snowfall (inches)

1 - 4   4 - 10   10 - 20   20 - 30   30+

February 15, 1958
Washington, D.C.

Copyright Washington Post;
Reprinted with permission of the D.C. Public Library

#10 Washington Snowstorm

The Snowstorm of February 15-16, 1958

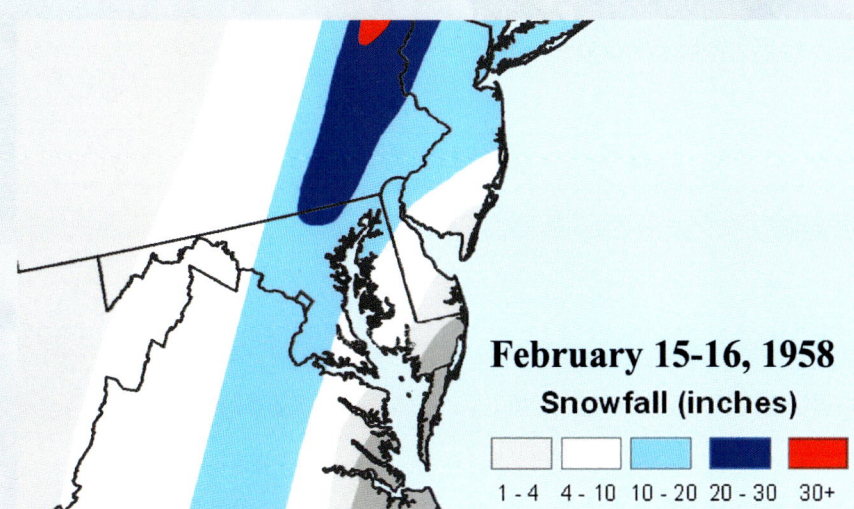

February 15-16, 1958
Snowfall (inches)

1-4 4-10 10-20 20-30 30+

D.C. Snow	14.4"
Area Snowfall Range	10-20"
D.C. Liquid	1.52"
Temperature Range	11-32 °F
Resulting Snow Cover	8 days
Season Total	40.4"

*The Capitol in snow.
February 6, 2010*

Ian Livingston

Chapter 3

Historic Snowstorms - A Photo Comparison with Snowmageddon

25

Digging out the car.
Washington, D.C.
January 28, 1922

Library of Congress

Digging out the car.
Washington, D.C.
February 19, 1979

Copyright Washington Post;
Reprinted with permission of the D.C. Public Library

Digging out the car.
Oakton, VA
February 7, 2010

Kevin Ambrose

Preparing to sled.
Washington, D.C.
January 28, 1922

Library of Congress

Preparing to sled.
Oakton, VA
February 6, 2010

Kevin Ambrose

Senate Page Snowball fight.
January 2, 1925

Library of Congress

Snowball fight near Connecticut Avenue.
March 29, 1942

Copyright Washington Post;
Reprinted with permission of the D.C. Public Library

Dupont Circle Snowball fight.
February 6, 2010

Antonio Zugaldia

The Korean War Memorial.
January 8, 1996

NOAA

The Korean War Memorial.
February 10, 2010

Michael Reynold/Corbis

The National Mall.
February 19, 2003

Kevin Ambrose

The National Mall.
December 22, 2009

Kevin Ambrose

The National Mall.
February 12, 2010

Kevin Ambrose

Washington street scene.
February 14, 1899
The Historical Society of Washington

Washington street scene.
The Taft Inauguration
March 4, 1909
Library of Congress

Washington street scene.
February 6, 2010
Ian Livingston

Pulling a sled near the Reflecting Pool.
January 13, 1912
Library of Congress

Sledding at the Capitol.
January 24, 1948
Copyright Washington Post;
Reprinted with permission of the D.C. Public Library

Sledding in Upper Marlboro, MD.
November 6, 1953
Copyright Washington Post;
Reprinted with permission of the D.C. Public Library

Pulling a basket near Capitol Hill.
March 3, 1978
Copyright Washington Post;
Reprinted with permission of the D.C. Public Library

Sledding down the Capitol Steps.
January 6, 1996
AP Photo/Cameron Craig

Snowboarding down the Lincoln Memorial Steps.
February 11, 2010
AP Photo/Jon Elswick

Washington, D.C.
January 28, 1922
Library of Congress

Washington, D.C.
February 16, 1958
Copyright Washington Post;
Reprinted with permission of the D.C. Public Library

Springfield, VA
January 31, 1966
Leedy Ambrose

Washington, D.C.
February 20, 1979
Copyright Washington Post;
Reprinted with permission of the D.C. Public Library

Frederick, MD
February 12, 1983
Copyright Washington Post;
Reprinted with permission of the D.C. Public Library

Fairfax, VA
January 8, 1996
Kevin Ambrose

Oakton, VA
February 19, 2003
Kevin Ambrose

Oakton, VA
December 19, 2009
Kevin Ambrose

Washington, D.C.
February 7, 2010
Ian Livingson

*Snow-covered Tidal Basin.
January 14, 1925*

Library of Congress

*Snow-covered Tidal Basin.
February 14, 2010*

Jim Schuyler

Driving in Washington.
January 28, 1922

Library of Congress

Driving in Arlington, VA.
January 30, 1966

Copyright Washington Post;
Reprinted with permission of the
D.C. Public Library

Driving in Washington.
February 10, 2010

Ian Livingston

A holiday decoration weighed down in snow, December 5, 2009.

Oakton, VA

Kevin Ambrose

December 5 snowmen in Washington. Washington, D.C. Ian Livingston

Chapter 4.

The December 5 Coincidence

Wayland Pond.
December 5, 2009

Kevin Ambrose

The December 5 Coincidence

The season's first snowstorm on December 5 brought an aburpt end to a long, mild autumn for the Washington region. Cold weather followed the snowstorm and National Airport's first freeze occurred on December 6. In retrospect, the early December snow was a good sign that a snowy winter was to follow.

D.C. Snow	0.2"
D.C. Rank	880 / 957
Area Snowfall Range	Trace - 7"
D.C. Liquid	.68"
Temperature Range	33-46 °F
Resulting Snow Cover	1 day
Season Total (to 12/5/2009)	0.2"

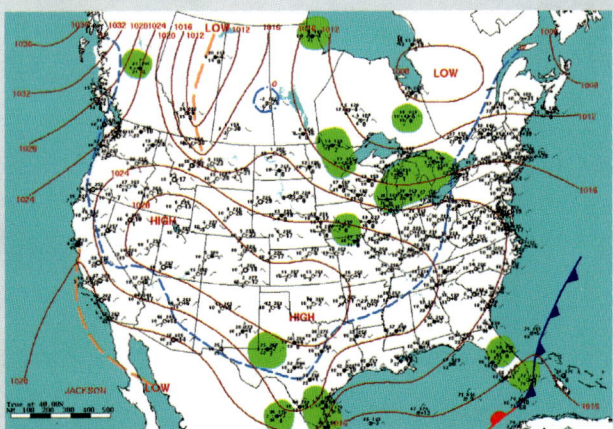 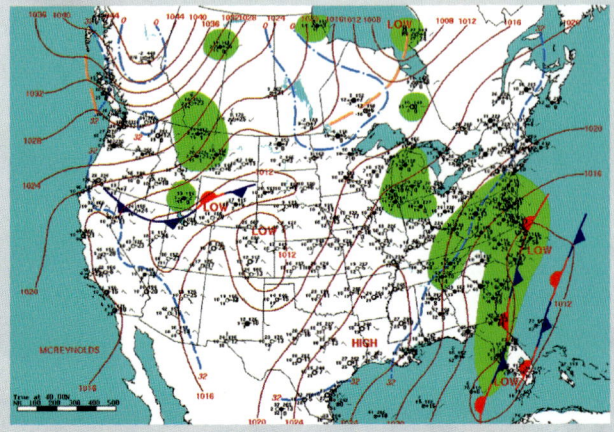

The surface weather maps for December 4, 2009 at 7 AM EST (left) and December 5, 2009 at 7 AM EST (right). - NOAA

For the fifth time in eight years, the Washington area experienced a snowstorm on December 5, 2009. It is unusual for Washington to see measurable snow in early December but it is quite amazing that the city received snowstorms on December 5 in five out of eight years ending 2009.

Since weather records began in Washington in 1871, there have been 180 storms with accumulating snow in December and 13 have occurred on December 5. Washington's largest December 5th snow occurred in 2002, with 6.1" of snow. A list of all years with December 5 snows include: 1893, 1902, 1904, 1910, 1921, 1926, 1954, 1984, 2002, 2003, 2005, 2007, 2009.

The snowstorm of December 5, 2009 began as rain across the Washington area but quickly changed to snow in the western suburbs. At the lower elevations, such as near the Potomac River, rain persisted for much of the storm. Accumulations ranged from 7" well to the west of town to 0.2" at National Airport. Common measurements were 2-4" across much of the northern and western suburbs with 1-2" in Washington and areas to the east and south of the city. It was a heavy, wet snowstorm, which is quite common for early in the winter season. It was also an elevation-dependent snowstorm, where even a few hundred feet above sea level made a difference between accumulating snow or just wet ground.

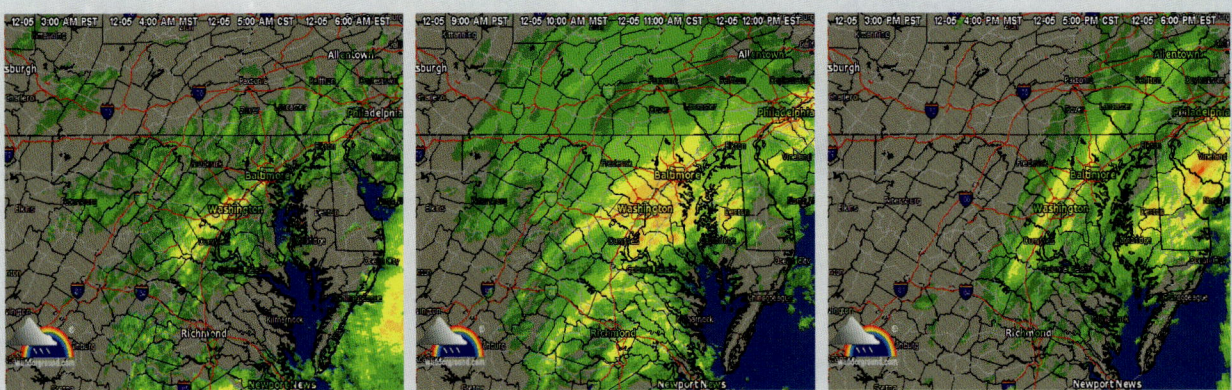

The radars for December 5, 2009 spanning 12 hours -- 6 AM EST (left), 12 PM EST (middle), and 6 PM EST (right).

http://www.wunderground.com/

Late-changing foliage in Washington during the season's first snowstorm, December 5, 2009.

Ian Livingston

A Few Other December 5 Snowstorms

*2003: The National Christmas Tree in snow.
December 5, 2003*

Kevin Ambrose

*2005: The White House in snow.
December 5, 2005*

Kevin Ambrose

*2007: The Capitol in snow.
December 5, 2007*

Kevin Ambrose

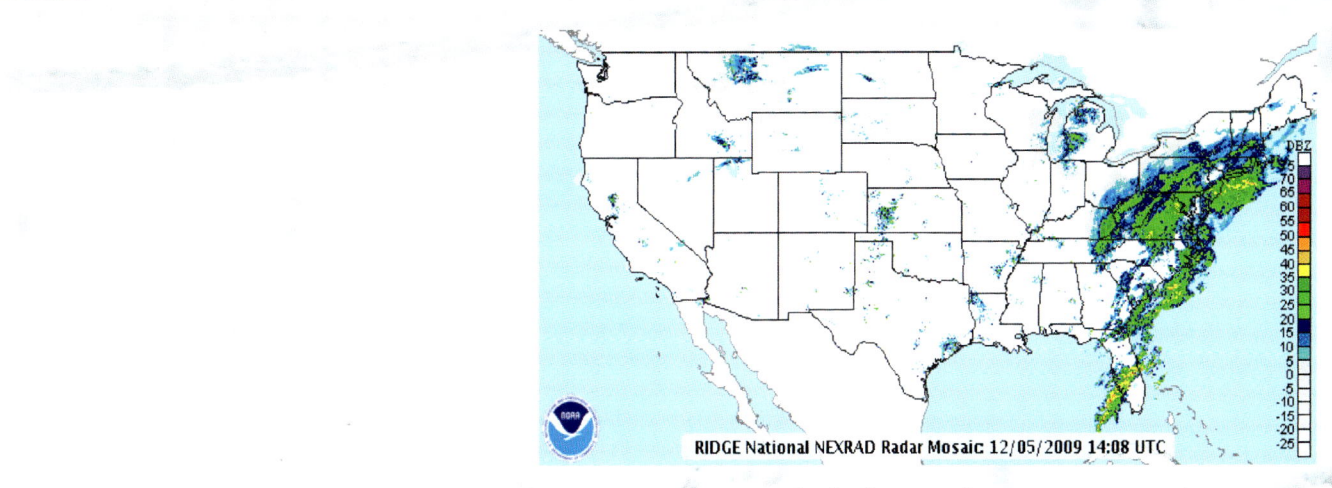

The national radar for December 5, 2009, 9 AM EST.
NOAA

Fun in the snow, Oakton, VA.
December 5, 2009
Kevin Ambrose

A snowy hike for groceries, December 20, 2009.

Ian Livingston

Cross-country skiing at the Jefferson.
December 19, 2009
AP Photo/Alex Brandon

Chapter 5.

Snowpocalypse - The Blizzard of December 18-19, 2009

*Washington, D.C.
December 19, 2009*

Ian Livingston

Snowpocalypse - December 18-19, 2009

A storm of the caliber of December 2009 easily equals or surpasses an entire average D.C. winter season in the matter of one or two days. What became the biggest snowstorm since 2003 not only made it into Washington's top 10 snowstorm list, setting a new December standard, it also followed a story line that would be closely repeated later in the historic winter of 2009-10.

D.C. Snow	16.4"
D.C. Rank	8 / 957
Area Snowfall Range	16-26"
D.C. Liquid	1.45"
Temperature Range	25-35 °F
Resulting Snow Cover	7 days
Season Total (to 12/19/09)	16.6"

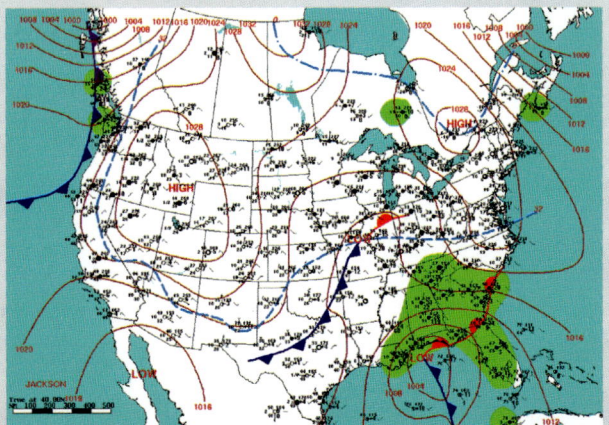 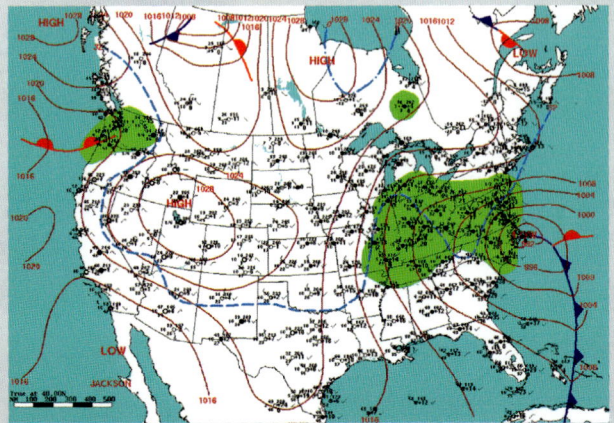

The surface weather maps for December 18, 2009 at 7 AM EST (left) and December 19, 2009 at 7 AM EST (right) - NOAA.

The tell-tale signs of winter 2009-10 were quick to show themselves -- it was going to snow at almost every real opportunity and area residents were going to be at the mercy of nature for extended periods. While the December 5 storm, that heavily favored the elevated western suburbs, could have been overlooked as pure coincidence, the major East Coast snowstorm to follow two weeks later was -- without question -- the "real deal."

A persistently strong "high-latitude blocking" pattern (one that sends cold into the area and slows a coastal storm keeping it from moving too far north), including a high pressure system over Greenland, helped prepare the stage for the storm. Other ingredients, including an interaction between the Pacific Ocean phenomenon El Nino's moisture-laden southern jet stream and an energetic low-pressure system hustling along through the northern United States, popped the proverbial cork.

The recipe created an explosive mixture that combined to spawn a strong coastal low pressure system which produced results not often seen in the Washington region, and never so early in the season.

Snowpocalypse started getting its act together on Thursday, December 17, 2009 as a large mass of moisture associated with a low pressure system forming in the Gulf of Mexico. Taking a classic track for an eventual monster East Coast snowstorm, it moved from near the Texas coast then up past Louisiana.

After traversing the Deep South, it swung toward the Carolina shore before heading northeast to a position off of Eastern New England and then departed out to sea. During this time its central pressure deepened through the 980s (mb) while it was east of the mid-Atlantic. Pressures of that level are roughly equivalent to those of a strong Category 1 hurricane.

While the Washington area anticipated the arrival of the storm on Friday the 18th, a state of emergency was declared in Virginia and a snow emergency was announced starting Saturday morning in Washington. States of emergency were eventually expanded for much of the region.

Snow moved in and started to accumulate across the area in the hours surrounding midnight on December 18th and 19th. At the same time, snow accumulated quickly to the south and west of the area and blizzard warnings were hoisted for Prince George's, Anne Arundel, and Calvert counties in Maryland. Much of the overnight snow was light to moderate but trending heavier. Several inches of fairly powdery snow were on the ground in the metro area by sunrise.

As Saturday morning wore on, the rapidly developing system off the North Carolina and Virginia coast began ejecting bands of blinding snow to the north across the region. National Airport reported heavy snow -- with visibilities as low as 1/8 of a mile. From 10 a.m. until 3:30 p.m. on Saturday the 19th, 6" of snow fell at National during, while other locations in the area saw even higher rates (as much as 2-3" per hour) accumulations.

Blizzard warnings were extended westward to the District on Saturday, but they did not end up verifying locally (sustained winds of 35 mph for three hours concurrent with reduced visibilities around 1/4 mile). The storm was either a true blizzard or close at a handful of coastal locations. Still, winds around the region were quite strong during the storm, with maximum sustained levels near 20 mph and gusts to around 30 mph. Moderate drifting was observed, especially in more rural locations after the storm's passage.

Light to occasionally moderate or heavy snow continued into Saturday evening as upper-level energy associated with the departing coastal low passed through the region from the west. Snow finally concluded overnight, over 24 hours after it began.

Incredibly, for the D.C. area at least, most spots (except well south and east) did not change over from snow to sleet or rain during the entire event. As far as big storms go in the region, this is a rarity. The area's proximity to the Atlantic Ocean and relatively southern latitude often promotes some warm-air intrusion which cuts down on totals. An example is the Presidents' Day storm of 2003 (number 6 all time), where snow turned to sleet in the immediate D.C. area and kept accumulations from reaching truly astounding levels.

Cold air was effectively funneled into the area thanks to the pattern setup that included a surface high pressure in Canada and other features including the Greenland Block referenced previously as well as an upper-level low pressure northeast of New England. This combination pushed air downward from the North Pole region and into the area. Temperatures remained in the mid-and-upper 20s for the entire accumulation portion of the event after only rising slightly above freezing on the 18th before snow began.

Additionally, big Washington area storms often produce dry slots (a portion of the storm lacking precipitation near the low center) over large regions where snow, sleet or rain will shut off during the height of a storm. During the Blizzard of 1996 (number 5 all time), a dry slot caused the snow to end for many hours. In Snowpocalypse, the dry slot stayed just east of the area, mainly impacting the Chesapeake Bay area eastward toward Delaware.

The storm ultimately dumped 16.4" of snow at National Airport making it -- at the time -- number 7 on the list of D.C. snowstorms. The Snowmageddon blizzard of February 2010 would later knock it back to number 8. The storm is also the largest ever in December, and it helped set a new D.C. December snowfall record of 16.6". The one-day snow total for December 19 ranks number 3 all time for one calendar day in D.C.

In other parts of the city, and the wider area, reports ranging from 18 to 26" were fairly numerous, including 20.5" in Arlington, VA, 24" in Bethesda, MD and 26.4" in Damascus, MD. At Baltimore-Washington International, a total of 21" fell with 20.5" coming in one calendar day, crushing the old one-day December record of 11.5". Dulles International picked up 19.3" with 16" coming in one day, also setting a new single-day December record.

Even though the storm occurred over a weekend, its effects lingered into the beginning of the following week for most people in the region, and even longer for some. Like the majority of Washington's largest snowstorms, the immediate aftermath of the storm saw the area struggle to regain a foothold after being truly crippled.

Significant segments of transportation remained at a standstill into Sunday the 20th. Area business, cultural and entertainment centers, as well as government and schools all struggled to get back to normal. Yet with stores eager to do business, last-minute Christmas shoppers with access to a vehicle that could withstand snowy road conditions were able to find many retailers open.

Hundreds of flights into area airports were cancelled during the storm and after, with at least temporary halts in all traffic reported. At National and Dulles, several runways were not cleared until Sunday.

All above-ground Metro stations, which closed as the storm pummeled the region on Saturday, remained shut through at least Sunday night. Metro bus lines were also suspended during the height of the storm and into Sunday morning, with some routes closed longer. Bus service was also stopped for the night on Sunday evening following the storm due to icy road conditions.

Even football was impacted by the snow. In Baltimore, officials were forced to push the Ravens' start time back to 4:15 p.m. from 1 p.m. to give crews enough of a chance to clear the stadium. Workers brought in by the Washington Redskins were graced with a Monday night game, but they had the task of removing an amazing 25 million pounds of snow (plus all the clearing of the parking lots).

After a Monday snow day, life more-or-less returned to normal by Tuesday as the federal government re-opened. Traffic and the commutes were, as usual following a big storm, nightmarish. Many area schools resumed as well, but others held off till later in the week or just gave in and started the holidays early. Places such as Loudoun County in Virginia added on almost a full extra week of winter vacation rather than even think about trying to open after the storm.

Compared to some snowstorms in the area like the first Presidents' Day storm in 1979 (number 3 all time), snow remained on the ground for a lengthy period afterwards. Much of the region held about one foot of snow cover through Tuesday the 22nd as daytime temperatures following the event were mainly in the mid-and-upper 30s and nighttime lows fell below freezing.

Those hoping for the not-so-common white Christmas in D.C. were rewarded -- at least when they woke up on the 25th. Only 13 years on record have had 1 inch or more of snow on the ground in D.C. on Christmas. The 7" on the ground at D.C. Christmas morning 2009 tied that of 1966 for the most on record. In 1962, 5.4" of snow fell on Christmas Day, the most on record in D.C.

The roughly one foot of snow that remained on the ground across the area on Christmas morning was mostly wiped out by a storm (mainly rain with some wintry mix) that occurred late in the day and into the next. Temperatures rising into the 50s ensured that by the 26th most locations were back to largely bare ground. Only snow piles, a few drifts and lots of memories were the remains of Snowpocalypse. For the next month, the active weather pattern would relax, but this was just the first major volley of the historic winter 2009-10.

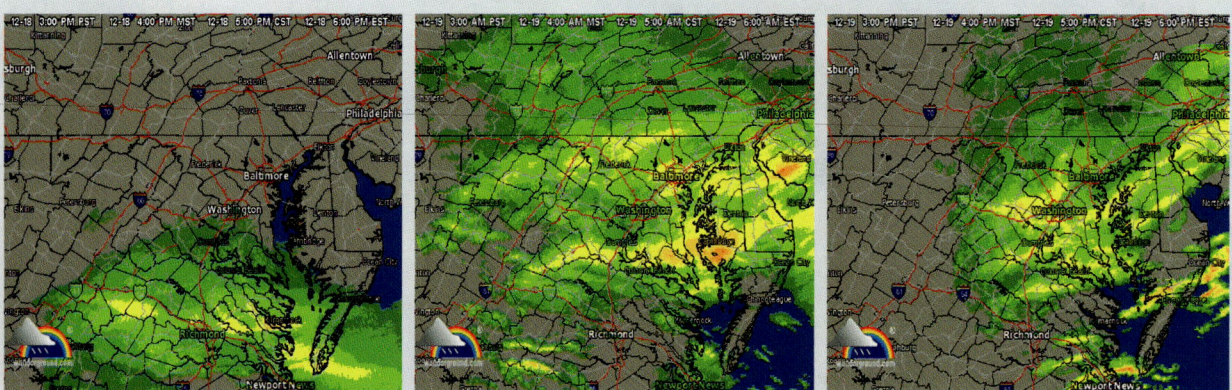

The radars for December 18-19, 2009, spanning 24 hours -- December 18 at 6 PM EST (left), December 19 at 6 AM EST (middle), and December 19 at 6 PM EST (right).

http://www.wunderground.com/

Heavy snow falls on the Capitol Christmas Tree.
December 18, 2009
Jim Walline

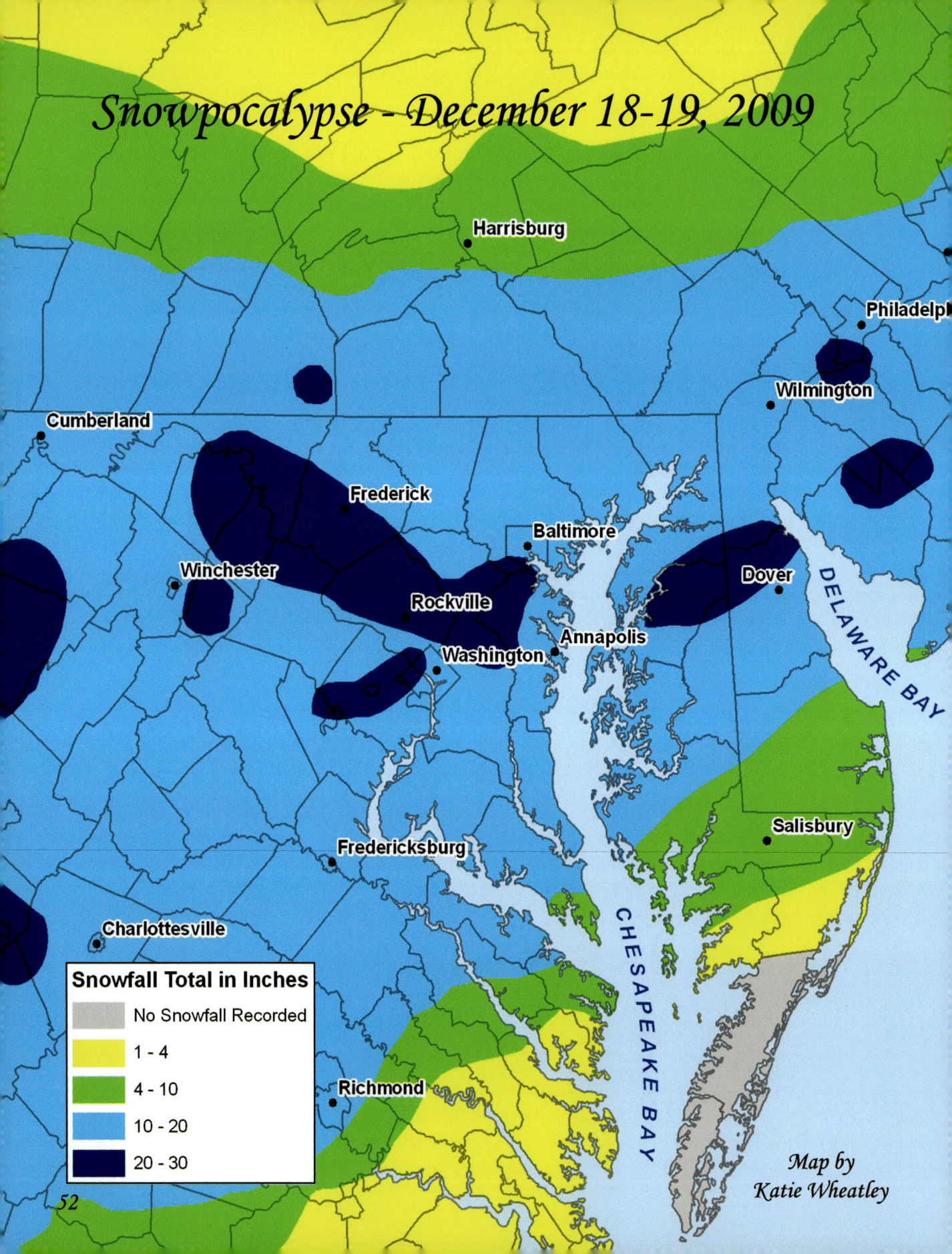

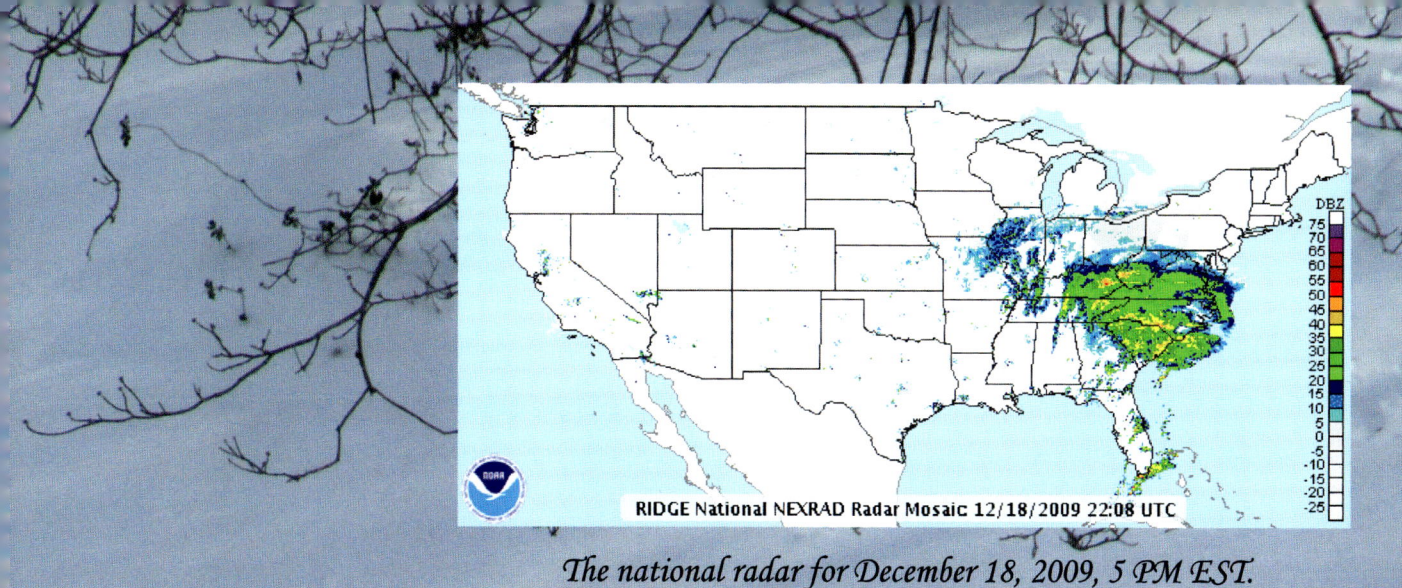

The national radar for December 18, 2009, 5 PM EST.
NOAA

Walking up the sledding hill.
Oakton, VA
December 21, 2009

Kevin Ambrose

The Capitol and Mall with snow.
December 22, 2009
Kevin Ambrose

The National Christmas Tree with Snow
December 22, 2009

Kevin Ambrose

A white Christmas Eve at Mount Vernon.
December 24, 2009

Kevin Ambrose

Mount Vernon with snow.
December 24, 2009
Kevin Ambrose

Snowman on the Mall.
December 20, 2009

Jim Schuyler

Snow-covered roads in Oakton, VA, January 9, 2010.

Kevin Ambrose

Chapter 6.

The Alberta Clipper of January 8, 2010

Sunrise in Oakton, VA, January 8, 2010.
Kevin Ambrose

The Tidal Basin at sunrise.
January 9, 2010
Kevin Ambrose

The Alberta Clipper of January 8, 2010

In some winters, a 1-2" event is memorable. Snow lovers in the area may have considered ritualistic dancing for such during the winters of 1972-73 and 1997-98, when only .1" of snow was measured at National Airport all season! During the winter of 2009-10, a storm like this is easily forgotten.

D.C. Snow	1.0"
D.C. Rank	589 / 957
Area Snowfall Range	1-2"
D.C. Liquid	0.03"
Temperature Range	23-32 °F
Resulting Snow Cover	1 day
Season Total (to 1/8/2010)	17.6"

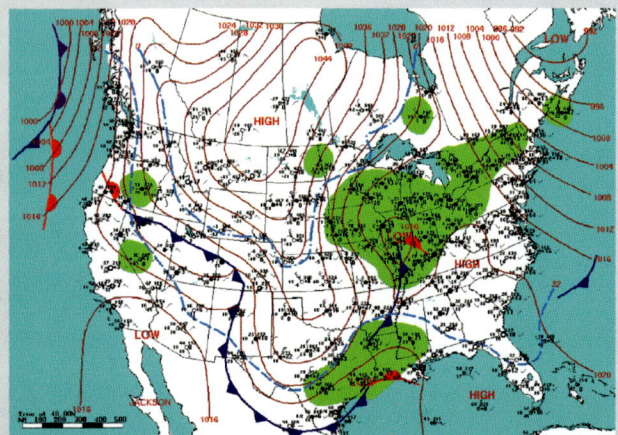 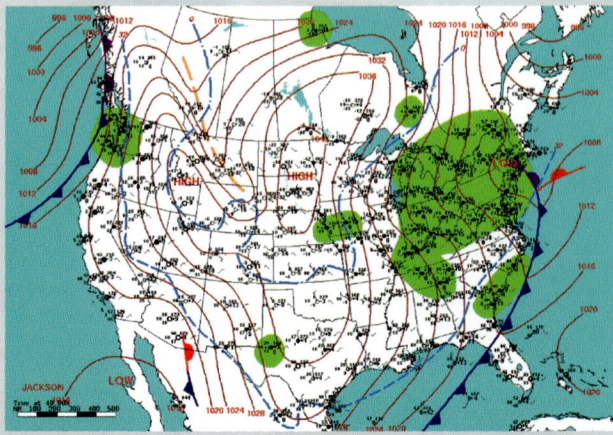

The surface weather maps for January 7, 2010 at 7 AM EST (left) and January 8, 2010 at 7 AM EST (right) - NOAA

Alberta Clippers are fast-moving, low pressure systems that move from southwestern Canada (often the province of Alberta) and track southeasterly across the Plains and into the Northeast or mid-Atlantic region. Due to their quick movement, and great distance from a moisture source, clippers usually result in light precipitation followed by a blast of cold air.

An Alberta Clipper like this one is a typical smaller-sized D.C. snow event. About 60 percent of all events with accumulating snow in Washington measure less than 2". Of course, many in that group also include storms that mixed or changed to rain and/or sleet. This particular storm went against the year-to-year norm and produced a best-case snow scenario for the Washington area.

The juicy southern jet stream that enhanced the December blockbuster, Snowpocalypse, headed south for the first half of January. Yet, the Greenland Block was still quite strong and cold air was dominant. However, moisture was lacking.

The Alberta Clipper passed right over the area -- a track that often includes a change to rain. However, this one came after dark, just before midnight, on the 7th, and continued through dawn on the 8th. The air accompanying it proved cold enough that most of the area ended up with a fairly fluffy 1-2" of snow, and a few locations neared 3". Following the storm, much of the end of January was mild, with temperatures reaching the upper 60s on the 25th. More winter was right around the corner though.

The national radar for January 7, 2010, 7 PM EST.
NOAA

The Jefferson Memorial and
a frozen Tidal Basin.

January 9, 2010

Kevin Ambrose

The Treasury Building, January 30, 2010.

Ian Livingston

Chapter 7.
The Snowstorm of January 30, 2010

Georgetown, January 30, 2010.
Kevin Ambrose

Georgetown.
January 30, 2010

Kevin Ambrose

The Snowstorm of January 30, 2010

On rare occasions, the entire Washington area will have temperatures in the teens and a winter storm will produce only powdery snow, without any mixed precipitation or rain. The snowstorm of January 30, 2010 was such a storm. The precipitation was forecast to be all snow across the entire Washington area, the only question was how much accumulation would be measured across the city and surrounding suburbs.

D.C. Snow	6.4"
D.C. Rank	88 / 957
Area Snowfall Range	4-9"
D.C. Liquid	0.33"
Temperature Range	18-23 °F
Resulting Snow Cover	7 days
Season Total (to 1/30/2010)	24.0"

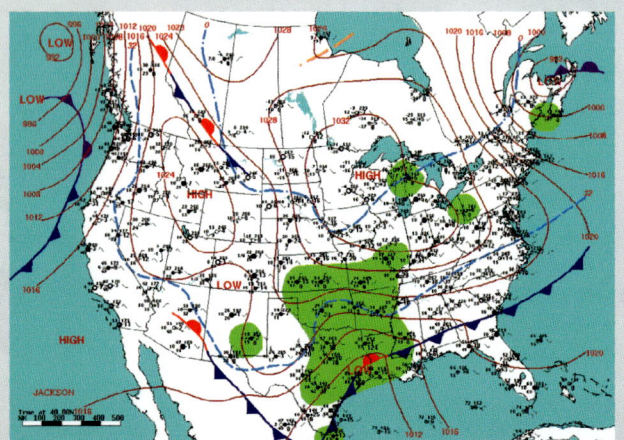 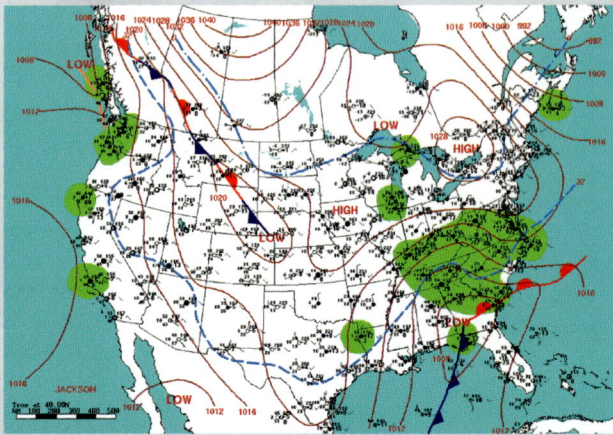

The surface weather maps for January 29, 2010 at 7 AM EST (left) and January 30, 2010 at 7 AM EST (right). - NOAA

Five days before the snowstorm, on January 25, weather models forecast a significant winter storm for the Washington area. The Global Forecast System (GFS) weather model showed a classic snowstorm setup. High pressure was parked to the north feeding cold air into the region while a coastal low pressure system already infused with El Nino moisture also began pulling in moisture from the Atlantic.

A day later, however, the weather models suddenly changed, taking the storm track well south of Washington. It appeared that Washington would be on the northern fringe of the storm, receiving light accumulations of snow, at best. (Computer weather models often do not lock onto a storm track until 2-3 days before the event). The storm was still 4 days away and the forecast track was changing with each model run.

Over time, the weather models began to trend the storm track back north, giving the area an increasing chance of significant snow.

Two days before the snowstorm, the forecast was for 1-2" of snow. One day before the storm, the forecast was increased to 1-4" of snow. On the day of the storm, the forecast was increased to 3-6" of snow. Ultimately, 6.4" of dry, powdery snow fell at National Airport. The high temperature only reached only 23 degrees and the cold temperature helped the snowfall measurements to be fairly uniform across the area.

The radars for January 30, 2010, spanning 6 hours -- 9 AM EST (left), 12 PM EST (middle), and 3 PM EST (right).
http://www.wunderground.com/

The Lincoln Memorial in snow, January 30, 2010.

Ian Livingston

The Korean War Memorial in snow, January 30, 2010.

Ian Livingston

A cold walk in the snow.
Washington, D.C.
January 30, 2010

Kevin Ambrose

The national radar for January 30, 2010, 6 AM EST.

NOAA

View from the Key Bridge
January 30, 2010
Kevin Ambrose

Wayland Park in Fairfax County.
February 3, 2010
Kevin Ambrose

Oakton, VA, February 3, 2010.
Kevin Ambrose

Chapter 8.

Snowmageddon's Appetizer - February 2-3, 2010

Wayland Park in Fairfax County, VA.
February 3, 2010

Kevin Ambrose

Snowmageddon's Appetizer - February 2-3, 2010

D.C. Snow	3.3"
D.C. Rank	245 / 957
Area Snowfall Range	2-5"
D.C. Liquid	.26"
Temperature Range	27-41 °F
Resulting Snow Cover	3 days
Season Total (to 2/3/2010)	27.3"

Already past seasonal average snowfall, some across the region were probably ready for a break. But, it was just the start of a storm barrage. Despite only moderately cold air that produced a wet and clingy snow, the second set of four winter storm warnings over a 12-day period verified easily.

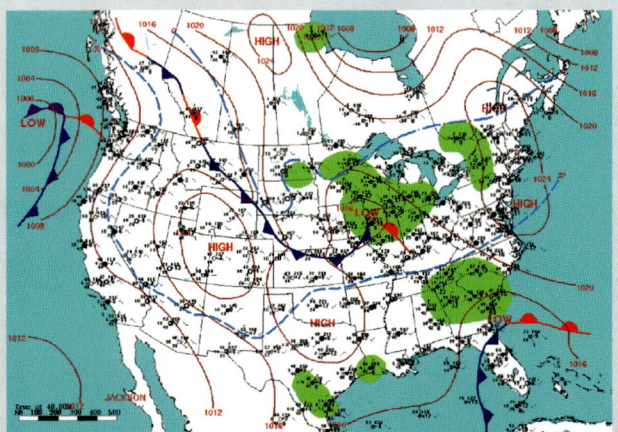 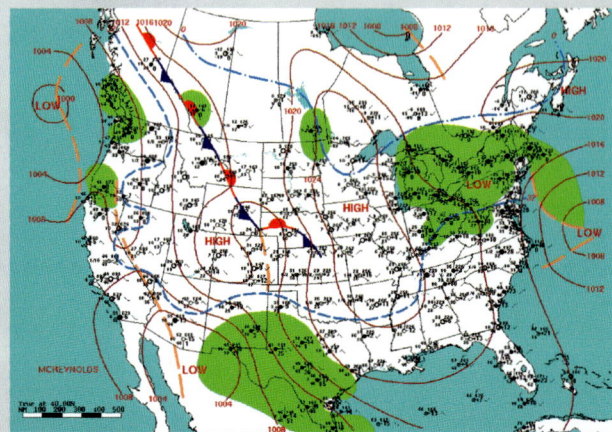

The surface weather maps for February 2, 2010 at 7 AM EST (left) and February 3, 2010 at 7 AM EST (right). - NOAA

While snow lovers rejoiced at the pattern, this storm -- only the 5th largest of 2009-10 in Washington -- did not disappoint. With snow events that arrive into marginal temperatures, several elements are often decisive across the area: nighttime snow, chillier air in advance, and some embedded heavier bursts. Snow already on the ground (from the January 30 storm) does not hurt either.

Several days out, this event was billed as a diffuse storm with much of the precipitation passing south and east of D.C. By early February 1, the trend toward a snowier outcome was apparent. As with most snowstorms during the winter of 2009-10, the ingredients for snow further aligned as the event neared.

Instead of limping harmlessly to the south as an undefined storm, an energetic southern system interacted with a weaker system passing through the northern U.S. This interaction created a coastal storm strong enough to send moisture north. Wet snow, which fell up to around 1" per hour for several hours, moved in around sunset and ended before dawn.

Almost lost in the ominous forecasts for another potential giant snowfall days later, this storm dropped a solid 3-6" snowfall across the wider region. National Airport's 3.3" was one of the lower totals, as usual, across the D.C. area. Temperatures at National remained near or above freezing for the entire event.

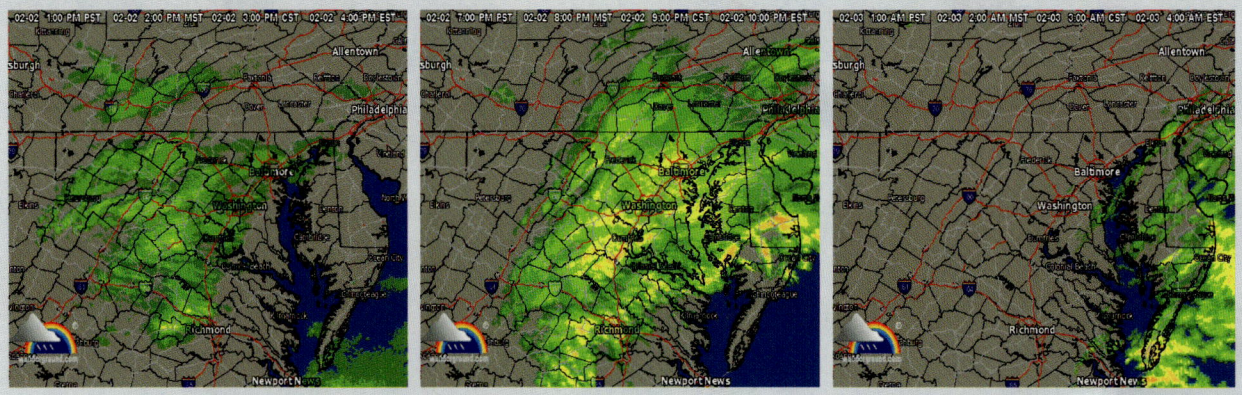

The radars for February 2-3, 2010, spanning 12 hours -- February 2 at 4 PM EST (left), February 2 at 10 PM EST (middle), and February 3 at 4 AM EST (right).

http://www.wunderground.com/

Arlington National Cemetery with snow, February 4, 2010.
Kevin Ambrose

View from the Capitol, February 6, 2010.

Ian Livingston

Chapter 9.

Snowmageddon - The Blizzard of February 5-6, 2010

*Supreme Court Building, February 6, 2010.
Ian Livingston*

The Capitol during Snowmageddon.
February 6, 2010

Ian Livingston

Snowmageddon - February 5-6, 2010

It is not often that snow accumulates on existing snow cover in D.C. It is also not common that Washington sees a snowstorm as moisture-laden or as well-forecast as this second, top 10 all time event of the 2009-10 season. A storm for the ages, Washington Post's Capital Weather Gang, and later President Obama, dubbed it D.C.'s "Snowmageddon."

D.C. Snow	17.8"
D.C. Rank	4 / 957
Area Snowfall Range	17-34"
D.C. Liquid	1.5"
Temperature Range	21-37 °F
Resulting Snow Cover	18 days
Season Total (to 2/6/2010)	45.1"

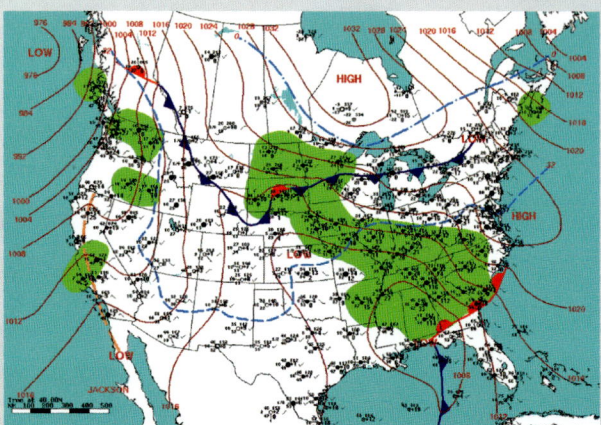 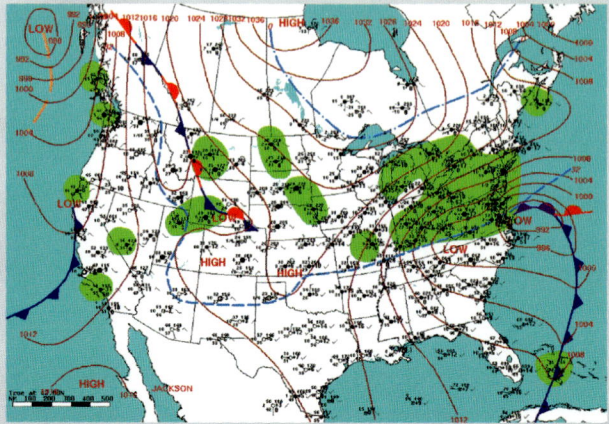

The surface weather maps for February 5, 2010 at 7 AM EST (left) and February 6, 2010 at 7 AM EST (right). - NOAA

Before 2010, almost no one would claim D.C. is a snowy place. Sure, there have been some snowy winters, like 1995-1996 and 2002-2003. Both of those winters -- and similar ones from days past -- were largely defined by one major storm and several moderate ones. Had that been the case, the December 2009 snowstorm was the main event of the season and area snow lovers would be left having to recall it for years to come. But after the end of January and during the first two weeks of February, it sure seemed like the D.C. area was relocated much further north, to a place like interior New England.

With the February 2-3 snow event barely out of the area, the ominous signs of a much larger system were growing stronger by the hour. A slow melt of the roughly 10-15" of snow that fell from January 30 to February 3 had insufficient to fully disappear before the next onslaught. In many places, there was still a decent snow cover when Snowmageddon began.

During the lead up to Snowmageddon, an enormous conglomeration of moisture with roots into the tropics traversed northern Mexico in the continued active, and El Nino enhanced, southern jet stream. Similar to the December storm, low pressure emerged around the Texas coast and moved to a position near Louisiana where it dropped 3-4" of rain.

From the Gulf of Mexico, the center of the storm transitioned to a position off the Southeast U.S. coast and tracked northeast to just off the North Carolina and Virginia shore by the morning of the Saturday the 6th. Also similar to the December snowstorm, the system was blocked from continuing too far north by cold high pressure in Greenland that funneled arctic air into the D.C. area during the course of the event. Instead of quickly passing by and heading north up toward New England, the storm slowly shifted east after pummeling the mid-Atlantic.

Thanks to the several similarities between the December 2009 storm and the February 5-6 snowstorm, the low pressure and extreme snowfall it produced were exceptionally well predicted as far as winter events go. The plume of moisture which dipped into the deep tropics only made forecasters more confident that a major event was on the verge of unfolding in and around D.C. A theme of 2009-10 -- increasing snow forecasts as the storm neared -- came to pass yet again with this event.

An expansive area of light snow moved into the D.C. area on the morning of Friday the 5th. In anticipation of the storm's arrival, most businesses, schools, and the federal government closed up shop early on Friday. Thanks in part to another major snowstorm on the 9th and 10th, the soonest many offices and schools would re-opened was one week later.

Initially, marginal temperatures near and just above freezing kept most accumulation to grassy surfaces or the coldest locations in the western suburbs. As the sun set on Friday the 5th, the snow's intensity picked up, while convective bands (similar to heavy rain patterns associated with thunderstorms) began to push into the area around the developing low pressure. Colder air aloft, continually reinforced by high pressure to the north, made this another somewhat rare storm in which almost all the precipitation fell as snow in the Washington area.

Periods of heavy snow, some accompanied by rolling thunder and obscured flashes of lightning, continued across the region late Friday evening through Saturday. Blizzard warnings were extended from the eastern shore back toward the west and into the District on Friday night. During the same period, Dulles Airport reported heavy snow every observation from 6 p.m. on the 5th until 8 a.m. on the 6th.

The storm came in two rounds for the D.C. area and points east. The first round was heavy and wet. The second -- caused by upper-level energy swinging across the region from the west -- also fell heavily, but it was drier and fluffier as temperatures dropped. Blizzard warnings, in effect for the city and places just northeast, did not verify locally as with the December 18-19 storm, but several locations near the coast did reach official criteria.

The storm, dubbed "Snowmageddon" by local and national media, and later President Barack Obama, dropped very significant snowfall across the entire Washington metro area. In most places the snow was chock-full of water content thanks to the tropical feed of the first portion of the storm. Snowmageddon rivaled the snowfall production of any other major snowstorm in recorded history; matters of where it fell on a top 10 list were largely defined by how the heaviest bands set up.

In addition to ranking number 4 all time for D.C., with 17.8" accumulation, the event ranks number 2 all time at the current observation location (National Airport). Much of the city reported totals in the 20 to 24 inch range, with the highest numbers located in a band just north and west of the city. Dulles Airport recorded an incredible 32.4" while places close by such as Leesburg, VA fell just short of 3 feet, with 34.5" reported.

Spots near Baltimore, through the northern D.C. suburbs and out toward the western D.C. suburbs received anywhere from 24 to 36". Regional spotters also reported as much as 2" or more of liquid equivalent water content in the snow, ranking Snowmageddon at the top of regional winter storms in that regard as well. The only major winter storms in D.C. history to drop more liquid equivalent in the city itself were the Knickerbocker storm of 1922 (number 1 all time) and the great February 1899 blizzard (number 2 all time).

Trees were not the only casualties. An hanger at Dulles Airport collapsed under the weight of the snow, as did several churches and firehouses across the area. Other facilities such as schools and businesses with flat-top roofs faced either partial or full roof collapse under the weight of the snow. The melt and freeze cycle that went into the next week also caused ice-damming issues such as icicles bringing down gutters or melt-water entering homes -- not too common for the area. All of these issues were exacerbated by the next storm.

The D.C. Metro was hit hard. Above-ground train service was suspended at 11 p.m. Friday the 5th. Bus service was stopped at 9 p.m. the same evening, and remained closed through the day Saturday and in "snow emergency" mode with limited operations through Monday. Some above-ground stations returned to service by Tuesday morning, while other lines (including many Blue Line stations) closed into and past Tuesday with the next storm bearing down.

All flights on Saturday the 6th from National Airport were canceled as were most flights at other local airports, with the main exceptions being international flights due to land during the storm. All area airports remained down through Sunday and even into Monday before slowly coming back into service, first with arrivals then with full operations.

With estimates of 500,000 tons of snow to clear in Virginia alone, snow plowing operations focused on primary roads and highways before targeting secondary thoroughfares and finally neighborhood locations. The first two objectives were not completed until late Sunday the 7th and late Monday the 8th, respectively. As neighborhoods began to see clearing operations on Tuesday, rumors of the next storm grew larger.

In many locations there was simply more snow than places to put it. Some neighborhoods and subdivisions (as with author Kevin Ambrose's residence in Oakton, Va.) would not see a plow until the second storm had come and gone, about a week after it all started.

Snowfall budgets were strained early and exceeded before the end of the season. For the first major snowstorm storm in December alone, D.C. used two-thirds of its annual budget. After several additional smaller events prior to Snowmageddon beginning, Maryland, Virginia and D.C. had already spent more than their annual budgets called for.

Even thought Snowmageddon was the second major storm of the winter and occurred on a weekend, its impacts were as extreme it gets in Washington. In addition to the normal slow-going tasks of clearing streets, rails, runways, and sidewalks of snow, the water-laden nature of the event caused numerous trees and power lines to fall. At the maximum, power was out for about 200,000 people in the broader metro area, and it would be at least mid-week before it returned for many. Unfortunately for area football fans awaiting big parties, the Super Bowl fell during that window.

Despite hardships from this dangerous storm, fun in the snow was still a story across the region. Sledders hit their favorite -- if not often used -- spots including Capitol Hill as well as numerous other hilly streets and parks. Snowball fights cropped up across parts of the city, with perhaps the largest a 2,000 person melee in Dupont Circle. Despite the near halt to normal everyday life, the beginning of "snow week 2010" was taken in stride by most. As the week drew on, some attitudes changed.

The federal government, along with numerous area businesses and schools, remained closed into the following week. As temperatures stayed in the chilly teens and 20s at night to low 30s during the day, allowing for little if any melting to help efforts.

By Monday the 8th, a storm expected to begin late on Tuesday and last through Wednesday was looking more and more intense on computer guidance, and local forecasts called for 5-10" additional snow. One of the most powerful northern jet stream storms of the winter was expected to collide with yet another piece of El Nino's moisture to create what would become a true blizzard across most of the area and cap off an incredible period of snow in the Washington region.

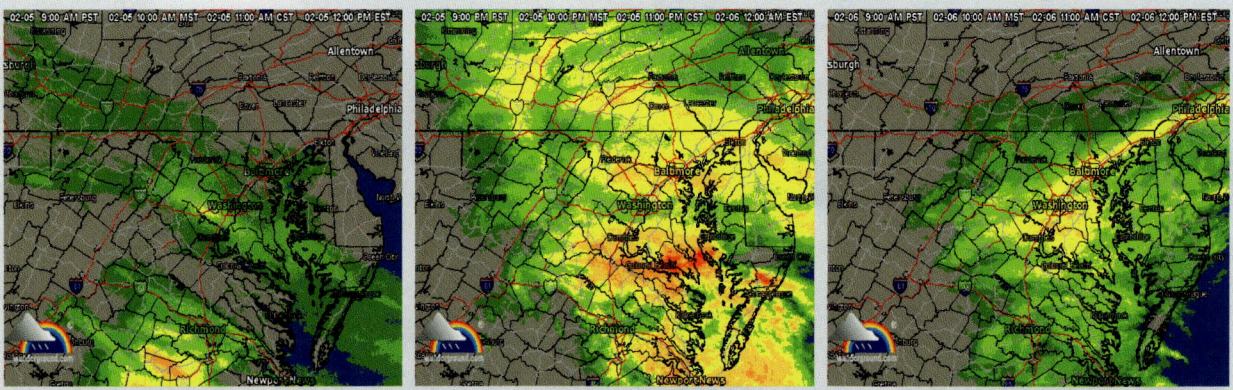

The radars for February 5-6, 2010, spanning 24 hours -- February 5 at 12 PM EST (left), February 6 at 12 AM EST (middle), and February 6 at 12 PM EST (right).

http://www.wunderground.com/

Georgetown covered in snow, February 6, 2010.

The United States Park Police

Arlington National Cemetary with snow, February 6, 2010.

The United States Park Police

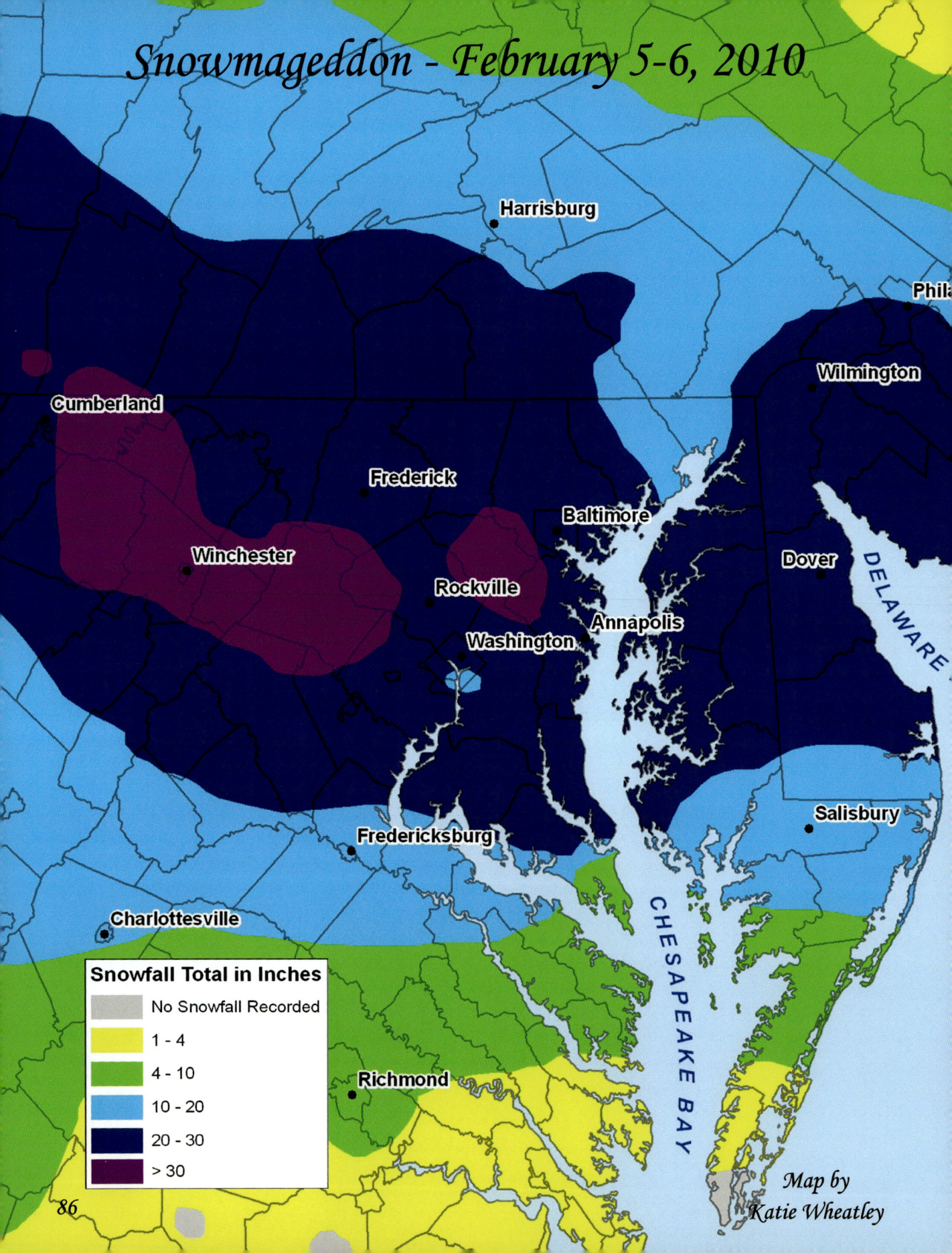

Snow accumulation in a basketball hoop after Snowmageddon.

Oakton, VA

February 7, 2010

Kevin Ambrose

Ulysses S. Grant Memorial.
Washington, D.C.
February 6, 2010
Ian Livingston

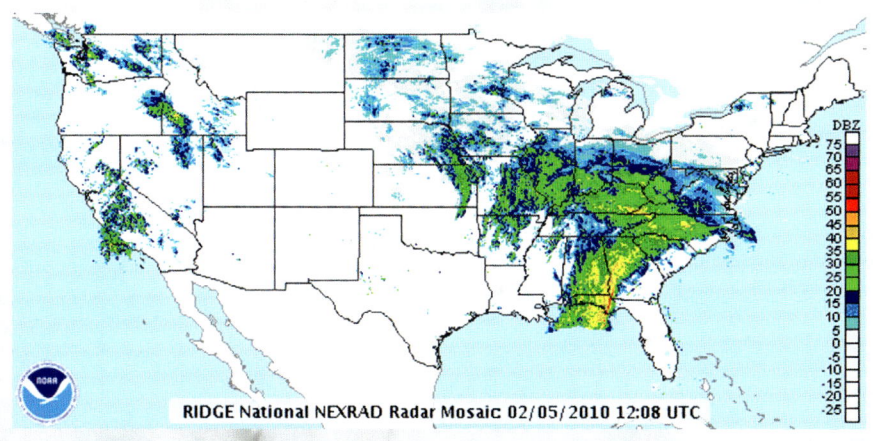

The national radar for February 5, 2010, 7 AM EST.
NOAA

A snow tunnel in Oakton, VA.
February 6, 2010
Kevin Ambrose

A mailbox is buried in snow during Snowmageddon.
Oakton, VA
February 6, 2010
Kevin Ambrose

Tree damage at the Senate Buildings. Fallen trees and limbs contributed to wide-spread power outages throughout the Washington area.

February 6, 2010

Ian Livingston

A large elm tree uprooted at the Tidal Basin, near the paddle boats. The heavy blanket of snow also damaged many of the cherry trees that grow along the Tidal Basin.

February 14, 2010

Jim Schuyler

Empty grocery shelves after Snowmageddon at the Safeway on 17th Street, near Dupont Circle.

February 7, 2010

Ed Whitaker

The Safeway at Maryland Avenue and Benning Road, NE. People who gave up waiting in massive lines left their groceries and supplies in shopping carts near the checkout lines.

February 8, 2010

Phil Yabut

A sign for VDOT snow plow operators in an Oakton neighborhood.

February 9, 2010

Kevin Ambrose

A sign to reserve a parking location in Cleveland Park.

February 13, 2010

Ian Livingston

The Jefferson Memorial after Snowmageddon.
February 7, 2010
The United States Park Police

Shoveling a driveway.
Oakton, VA
February 7, 2010
Kevin Ambrose

Connecticut Avenue, February 10, 2010.

Ian Livingston

*Blizzard Conditions in Washington.
February 6, 2010*

Ian Livingston

Chapter 10.

Snoverkill -
The Blizzard of February 9-10, 2010

Blizzard conditions in Washington.
February 10, 2010

Ian Livingston

Snoverkill - February 9-10, 2010

While the Capital region was still digging out from the "Snowmageddon" days prior, area forecasters began talking about yet another snowstorm to come. Snow totals for this event ended up less than the previous big storms of winter 2009-10 in the D.C. metro, but winds were brutal and it added another layer to an already hefty snow pack. As the once in a lifetime series of events came to a close, 25-45" of snow lay across the region.

D.C. Snow	10.8"
D.C. Rank	24 / 957
Area Snowfall Range	7-27"
D.C. Liquid	.63"
Temperature Range	20-31 °F
Resulting Snow Cover	14 days
Season Total (to 2/10/2010)	55.9"

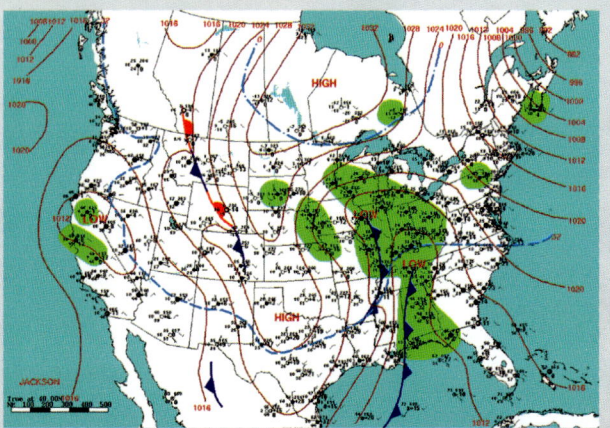 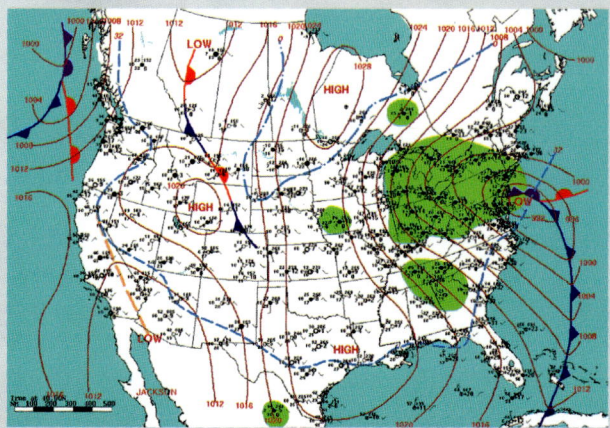

The surface weather maps for February 9, 2010 at 7 AM EST (left) and February 10, 2010 at 7 AM EST (right). - NOAA

Somewhat unlike the previous major snowstorms to hit the D.C. area during the winter of 2009-10, Snoverkill got most of its power from a storm originating in Canada. Like the others, interactions between the northern and southern jet streams created an atypically powerful storm. On the morning of Monday the 8th of February, a strong upper-level low pressure was diving southeast through Minnesota on a track that brought it through the Midwest and past Chicago.

Meanwhile, snow that was still not cleared in many streets hardened in advance of more to come. Huge snow piles and numerous icy surfaces kept people from moving easily in most cases or safely in others. Overall, most tasks involved in clearing the first large storm were slow, even by area standards as temperatures remained cold. Drifts over roads and rails, lack of spots to put snow, and growing public agitation with the series of events all added to growing frustration across the region.

It is basically unheard of for D.C. to get two powerhouse storms over such a short period of time and 4 snowstorms total in less than two weeks. Local establishments such as grocery stores, restaurants, and bars cleaned out in the earlier rush, continued began to run low on supplies during the days of being snowed-in following Snowmageddon. As the February 9-10 snowstorm was approaching, deliveries remained sparse. Widespread shortages of certain foods -- and even worse, beer -- were reported across the area.

The weather pattern cared not. The northern U.S. storm that was traveling southeast merged with another smaller system in the still constant supply line of El Nino induced southern jet stream moisture. The separate storms combined to spawn a new and dynamic low pressure off the Carolina coast that then crawled north to a position east of Delaware. The storm ultimately ran into the persistent Greenland Block and drifted eastward out to sea while deepening to the strength of a Category 1 hurricane.

The snow emergency in D.C., previously lifted for the city early on Monday the 8th, was reinstated on Tuesday the 9th as the new storm moved toward the region. Local media described the series of snowstorms as a natural disaster. And while snow is often viewed as beautiful, or even magical, few across the area would argue with the usage of such words as the week wore on.

While Snoverkill moved toward the region, the federal government announced a highly unusual 3rd day in a row of full closure. The only previous time this happened because of weather-related reasons was following the Blizzard of 1996. Ultimately, the federal government would stay closed through all of Thursday the 11th as well, making it the longest closure due to weather in history at 4 full days. Only the budget impasses of 1995 and 1996 kept federal workers at home for a longer period of time.

Bands of snow that moved into the D.C. area late on Tuesday the 9th accumulated quickly and amounted to several inches prior to midnight. The first part of the event eventually saw a transition to sleet and freezing rain across a good portion of the region. After a general lull through the early morning of the 10th, with batches of light mixed precipitation interspersed, intense snow banding developed to the west of the coastal low center -- right over the metro area -- around sunrise.

As blinding snow expanded over the region in response to the deepening low pressure, so did the wind's ferocity. Blizzard warnings were issued for the entire metro area and winds created true whiteout conditions for portions of the rest of the day. National Airport recorded a maximum wind gust of 46 mph, Dulles Airport hit 47 mph, and Baltimore-Washington International topped 40 mph. In Manassas, Va., an unofficial wind gust to 60 mph was recorded.

While the start of the storm featured some brief warming of the air mass, the snow on Wednesday the 10th was accompanied by very cold air. Temperatures near 30 around sunrise dropped into the teens by early afternoon before rebounding into the low 20s as snow wound down. In the Washington area, and to the northeast, snow continued moderately to heavily through the morning before tapering in the afternoon and departing in the evening. Areas west of the Beltway saw a quicker end to the snow in this storm, while it lingered considerably longer east.

New snow accumulation across the D.C. area ranged from around half a foot over western sections to 15" or a little more to the east and northeast. Up to and past 2 feet of new snow was reported across northern Maryland. Though not quite on par with the earlier events of the season in the immediate metro area as far as accumulation goes, the 10.8" measured at National Airport puts the storm in the top 25 snowstorms in recorded history for Washington.

No season other than 2009-10 has featured three top 25 storms -- 1898-99 (the number 2 winter all time) and 1857-58 had two such storms each. All other events on the top 25 list were the only occurrence in a given winter.

By the storm's conclusion, counties in the immediate D.C. area saw drifts 4 to 6 feet tall or higher and anywhere from 25" to 40" or more of snow on the ground from the two storms combined. Further north in Maryland, drifts higher than 6 feet occurred and some spots finished off the back-to-back storms with over 50" of snow on the ground.

The blizzard pushed all three local climate locations to their snowiest seasons on record. D.C. surpassed the previous record of 54.4" in 1898-99 early in the afternoon – between 1 p.m. and 2 p.m. -- of the 10th. It finished the season with 56.1" of snow. Baltimore-Washington International finished the season with 77" of snow, and Dulles International finished with 73.2".

In addition to the seasonal records being broken by this storm, it also helped set other records. The 28.6" of snow recorded officially in D.C. made for the snowiest week in recorded history. Baltimore also broke the record for its snowiest month ever with 50" total, 49.5" of which fell during the first ten days of the month. Dulles set a new record for snowiest month as well with 46.1" of snow during February.

While the blizzard pounded the area, transportation was again brought to a standstill. And this time the standstill was all encompassing for several hours before easing to a lesser standstill afterwards. During the height of the storm on Wednesday the 10th, visibilities near zero (in feet) caused municipalities to call their plows from roads due to unsafe conditions. Regional train service was halted, and those who wanted to go outside were forced to fend for themselves if they were willing to take the chance. At least two dozen people were reported stranded on roadways in Frederick County, MD alone.

Airports, which just reopened following cleanup from the previous storm, were forced to shut down again on Wednesday. They were able to reopen for flights during the morning of Thursday the 11th. Southwest Airlines reported more cancellations of flights due to weather during the back-to-back snowstorms than at any other time during the company's history. Service did not return to "normal" until Friday the 12th, and some delays persisted into the weekend.

Public transportation remained hard hit across the area as the storm arrived and only got worse by completion. Above-ground Metro rail returned to full service on all but the Blue Line as snow began to fall late on Tuesday. On Wednesday it was back to just underground rail service. Additional clearing capabilities streaming into the city following the series of storms would prove to quicken the process going forward.

All above-ground Red Line train service was restored by late in the afternoon on Thursday the 11th. Other stations remained closed until the next morning when the majority of the workforces in D.C. returned to their offices for the first time in a week. The return to work would prove to be a nightmare as massive, now reinforced, snow piles remained on main roads and various bus lines continued to have trouble navigating hills and side streets.

Even the U.S. Postal Service cancelled deliveries for an unprecedented second time in a week as the storm raged on Wednesday. No mail deliveries occurred in Washington, Maryland and most of Northern Virginia. Officials could not remember such suspensions in recent history.

There are certain commonalities in Washington's biggest snowstorms. One is area transplants who came from further north making fun of the city's ability to deal with snow. After the first big February event there were still some out there saying "Oh, this is nothing compared to…", but looking out the window during and after Snoverkill helped change their tune. Maybe it was the week of being largely stranded in place or maybe it was the seeming transformation of Washington into Alaska.

The period after the blizzard saw an abrupt end to the snowfall of the winter season. Temperatures remained chilly but not frigid in the week following the storm. In D.C., snow on the ground dwindled to less than a foot within a week, while the suburbs held deeper snow a bit longer. All the snow pack from the record onslaught of wintry weather melted by 14 to 18 days later, but some spots saw snow cover for almost one full month.

The winter concluded tamely with a quick flip to warm conditions by March which lasted through the record hot summer of 2010. Before that came to pass, the final tale of winter 2009-10 was snow piles. Towering everywhere after the back-to-back snowstorms, they continued to dot most of the region into March despite warming weather. Amazingly enough, some piles that were created next to large structures such as a parking garage at Baltimore-Washington International lasted all the way into early May -- almost 6 months to the day after the first flakes of the winter fell.

The radars for February 9-10, 2010, spanning 24 hours -- February 9 at 7 PM EST (left), February 10 at 8 AM EST (middle), and February 10 at 7 PM EST (right).

http://www.wunderground.com/

Cars buried in snow in Cleveland Park, D.C.

February 10, 2010

Ian Livingston

*A wall of snow blocks a road in Oakton, VA.
This is the location where a snow plow gave up
trying to clear the streets two days earlier.*

February 10, 2010

Kevin Ambrose

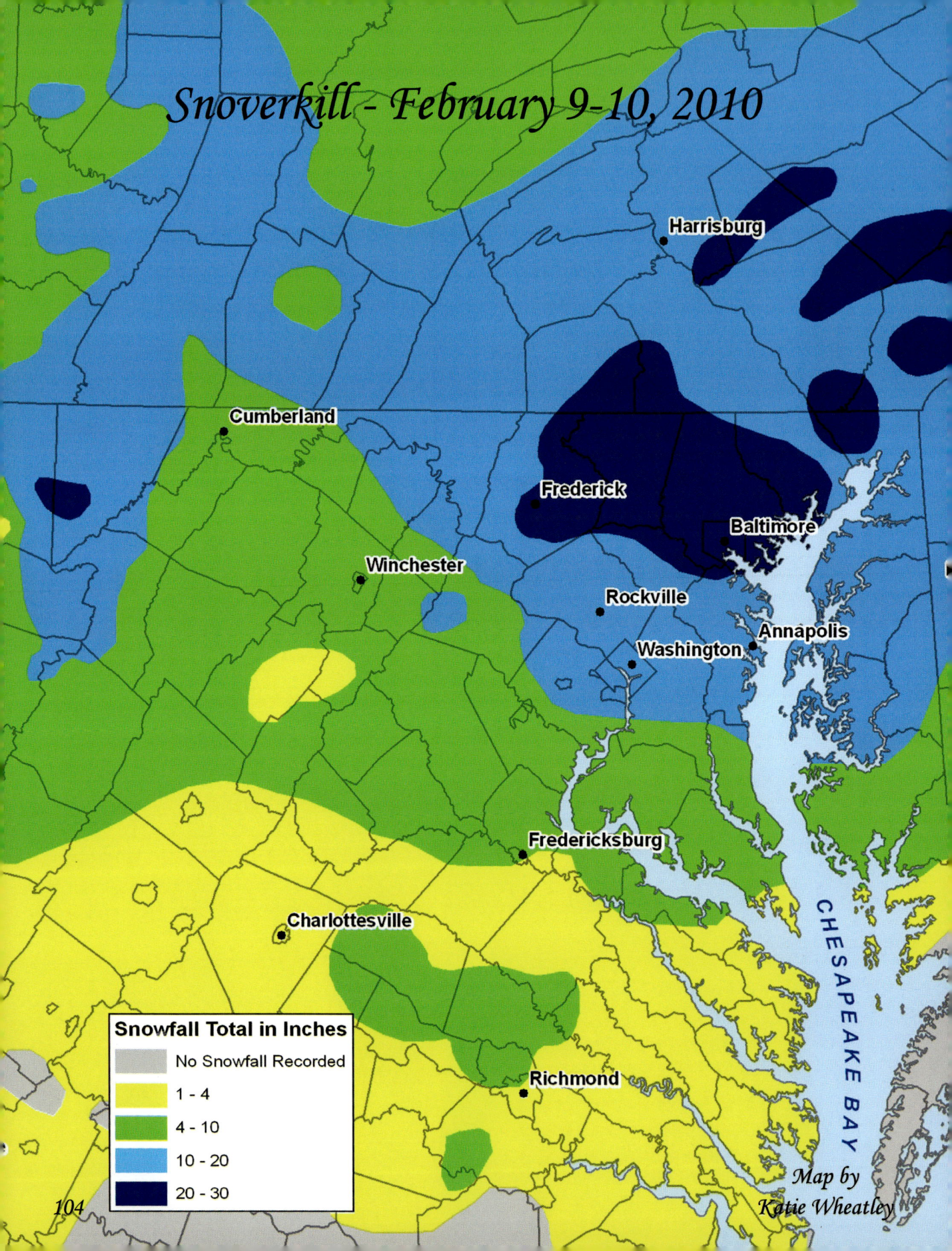

Shoveling in Washington, D.C.
February 10, 2010
Ian Livingston

The Mall after the blizzards.
February 12, 2010

Kevin Ambrose

The national radar for February 9, 2010, 7 PM EST

NOAA

The Mall after the blizzards.
February 12, 2010

Kevin Ambrose

Ice dams occurred on many houses and buildings in the Washington area after the blizzards. Ice dams are ridges of ice that form along the edge of a roof, blocking melting snow from properly draining off of a roof. The icicles can grow very large and break free from their own weight.

February 10, 2010

Ian Livingston

Metrorail was curtailed to underground stations during the blizzards. This photo was taken from a metro train near East Falls Church on February 12, 2010, when the above ground stations of the Orange Line reopened.

February 12, 2010

Kevin Ambrose

Washington, D.C.
February 13, 2010
Ian Livingston

Snow piles lasted well into March and April across the Washington area. A snow pile in Charlottesville, VA named Mt. Chipotle lasted until April 28 and a snow pile at BWI Airport lasted until May 3.

Vienna, VA.
March 5, 2010
Kevin Ambrose

*Snow piles at the Fair Oaks Mall.
Fairfax, VA
March 6, 2010
Kevin Ambrose*

Acknowledgments

A special thanks to the following organizations for providing content and/or photographs:

- Associated Press
- Capital Weather Gang
- Corbis
- Martin Luther King Library
- NASA
- NOAA
- The Historical Society of Washington
- The Library of Congress
- The United States Park Police
- The Washington Post
- Weather Underground

A special thanks to the following individuals for providing content and/or photographs:

- Jason Samenow
- Jim Schuyler
- Jim Walline
- Katie Wheatley
- Ed Whitaker
- Phil Yabut
- Antonio Zugaldia

Blizzard scene in Washington.
February 10, 2010
Ian Livingston

Bibliography

Ambrose, Kevin. Blizzards and Snowstorms of Washington, D.C., Historical Enterprises, 1993.

Ambrose, Kevin; Henry, Dan; Weiss, Andy. Washington Weather, Historical Enterprises, 2002.

Ambrose, Kevin. "The Perfect Snowstorm," Capital Weather Gang, December 20, 2009. Accessed at: http://voices.washingtonpost.com/capitalweathergang/2009/12/the_perfect_snowstorm.html

Armao, Jo-Ann. "Okay maybe Washington is experiencing a blizzard," Post Partisan, February 10, 2010. Accessed at: http://voices.washingtonpost.com/postpartisan/2010/02/okay_maybe_washington_is_exper.html

Bartlett, Anne. "Rail service extended to above-ground stations," Post Now, February 8, 2010. Accessed at: http://voices.washingtonpost.com/local-breaking-news/traffic-and-transportation/slow-going-this-morning-even-w.html

Bell, Ian; Visbeck, Martin. "North Atlantic Oscillation," via columbia.edu. Accessed at: http://www.ldeo.columbia.edu/res/pi/NAO/

Berman, Mark. "Airports open – for now," Get There, February 9, 2010. Accessed at: http://voices.washingtonpost.com/getthere/2010/02/airports_open_--_for_now.html

Bolden, Michael. "BWI opens one runway," Get There, February 7, 2010. Accessed at: http://voices.washingtonpost.com/getthere/2010/02/according_to_a_spokesman_the.htm

CoCoRaHS, "Station Snow Summary Report," includes snowfall totals for seasonal map, as of 2010. Accessed at: http://www.cocorahs.org/ViewData/StationSnowSummary.aspx

Halsey III, Ashley. "In D.C. area, outages, snow plowing conspire against normal week ahead," The Washington Post, February 7, 2010. Accessed at: http://www.washingtonpost.com/wp-dyn/content/article/2010/02/06/AR2010020603022.html

Halsey III, Ashley; Weil, Martin. "Snowstorm's intensity has D.C. region hunkering down," The Washington Post, February 6, 2010. Accessed at: http://www.washingtonpost.com/wp-dyn/content/article/2010/02/05/AR2010020501308.html

Halsey III, Ashley; Zapotosky, Matt. "Washington region digs out, but more snow ahead Tuesday," The Washington Post, February 8, 2010. Accessed at: http://www.washingtonpost.com/wp-dyn/content/article/2010/02/07/AR2010020701100_pf.html

Halsey III, Ashley. "With snow approaching, Washington area officials wonder how to pay for plowing," The Washington Post, February 5, 2010. Accessed at: http://www.washingtonpost.com/wp-dyn/content/article/2010/02/04/AR2010020403074_pf.html

Halverson, Jeffrey B.; Rabenhorst, Thomas D. "The Mid-Atlantic's Blockbuster Winter of 2009-10," Weatherwise, July/August 2010.

Johns Hopkins University Advanced Physics Laboratory, "March 2010 Summary," includes seasonal snowfall totals for map, March 2010. Accessed at: http://www.jhuapl.edu/weather/education/ACON Files/2010Mar_Summary.pdf

Junker, Wes. "Why was last year so snowy? Part I and II," Capital Weather Gang, November 1-2, 2010. Accessed at: http://voices.washingtonpost.com/capitalweathergang/2010/11/why_was_last_year_so_snowy_par.html; http://voices.washingtonpost.com/capitalweathergang/2010/11/why_was_last_year_so_snowy_par_1.html

Kocin, Paul J.; Uccellini, Louis W. Northeast Snowstorms, American Meteorological Society, 2004.

Livingston, Ian. "PM Update: Melt, freeze, repeat…," Capital Weather Gang, December 21, 2009. Accessed at: http://voices.washingtonpost.com/capitalweathergang/2009/12/pm_update_the_melt_freeze_melt.html

Livingston, Ian. "How much snow did you get in 2009-10?," Eastern U.S. Weather Forums, October 2010. Accessed at: http://www.easternuswx.com/bb/index.php?/topic/239222-how-much-snow-did-you-get-in-2009-10/

Livingston, Ian. "The evolution of a monster D.C. area snowstorm," Capital Weather Gang, December 22, 2010. Accessed at: http://voices.washingtonpost.com/capitalweathergang/2009/12/images_of_a_monster_east_coast.html

Livingston, Ian. "The incredible output of Snowmageddon," Capital Weather Gang, February 8, 2010. Accessed at: http://voices.washingtonpost.com/capitalweathergang/2010/02/the_evolution_of_snowmageddon.html

Morello, Carol; Halsey III, Ashley. "Historic snowstorm in D.C. leaves a mess to be reckoned with", The Washington Post, February 7, 2010. Accessed at: http://www.washingtonpost.com/wp-dyn/content/article/2010/02/06/AR2010020600683_pf.html

National Climatic Data Center, "Arctic Oscillation (AO)," National Oceanic and Atmospheric Administration (NOAA), 2010. Accessed at: http://www.ncdc.noaa.gov/teleconnections/ao/

National Climatic Data Center. "Daily Observational Data for D.C. (DCA), Dulles (IAD) and Baltimore (BWI)," NOAA, historical record as of 2010.

National Climatic Data Center. "The Northeast Snowfall Impact Scale (NESIS)," NOAA, 2010, Accessed at: http://www.ncdc.noaa.gov/snow-and-ice/nesis.php

National Weather Service Baltimore/Washington. "D.C. area climate statistics," as of 2010. Accessed at: http://www.weather.gov/climate/index.php?wfo=lwx

National Weather Service Baltimore/Washington. "DCA/IAD/BWI all set seasonal snowfall records," via easternuswx.com, February 10, 2010. Accessed at: http://www.easternuswx.com/bb/index.php?/topic/224489-dcaiadbwi-all-set-seasonal-snowfall-records/

National Weather Service Baltimore/Washington. "Event Page Compilation," includes storm totals and maps of 2009-10 events, as of 2010. Accessed at: http://www.erh.noaa.gov/lwx/events/

O'Keefe, Ed. "Eye Opener: Mail service suspended in D.C. area," Federal Eye, February 10, 2010. Accessed at: http://voices.washingtonpost.com/federal-eye/2010/02/eye_opener_postal_service_repo.html

O'Keefe, Ed. "Federal government shutdown extends to Thursday," Federal Eye, February 10, 2010. Accessed at: http://voices.washingtonpost.com/federal-eye/2010/02/federal_government_shutdown_ex.html

Rogers, Matt. "How did this happen? Blame the North Pole and the equator," Capital Weather Gang, December 21, 2009. Accessed at: http://voices.washingtonpost.com/capitalweathergang/2009/12/how_did_this_happen.html

Schulte, Brigid. "Is your grocery store cleaned out?," Story Lab, February 9, 2010. Accessed at: http://blog.washingtonpost.com/story-lab/2010/02/is_your_grocery_store_cleaned.html

Samenow, Jason. "Alert: Serious snow/wind risk late Tuesday into Wed," Capital Weather Gang, February 8, 2010. Accessed at: http://voices.washingtonpost.com/capitalweathergang/2010/02/alert_serious_snowwind_a_risk.html

Samenow, Jason. "Snowstorm blossoming, some sleet south," Capital Weather Gang, February 5, 2010. Accessed at: http://voices.washingtonpost.com/capitalweathergang/2010/02/snow_storm_blossoming_some_sle.html

Samenow, Jason. "Unbelievable: Still snow at BWI…," Capital Weather Gang, May 4, 2010. Accessed at: http://voices.washingtonpost.com/capitalweathergang/2010/05/unbelievable_still_snow_at_bwi.html

Samenow, Jason; Posegate, Ann. "Washingtonians react to storm and storm stats," Capital Weather Gang, December 20, 2009. Accessed at: http://voices.washingtonpost.com/capitalweathergang/2009/12/video_washingtonians_react_to.html

Shaver, Katherine. "Southwest: Full service at BWI Friday," Get There, February 11, 2010. Accessed at: http://voices.washingtonpost.com/getthere/2010/02/reagan_national_reopens_for_fl.html

Stewart, Nikita. "D.C. to reinstate snow emergency at 4 p.m.," D.C. Wire, February 9, 2010. Accessed at: http://voices.washingtonpost.com/dc/2010/02/dc_to_reinstate_snow_emergency.html

Storm Prediction Center. "Mesoscale Discussion 104 – Referring to 1-3"/hr snow over area," NOAA, February 5, 2010. Accessed at: http://www.spc.noaa.gov/products/md/md0104.html

Tedford, Deborah; Gonzales, Richard; Smith, Robert. "East Coast Digs Out From Record Snow", National Public Radio, February 10, 2010. Accessed at: http://www.npr.org/templates/story/story.php?storyId=123558638

Thompson, Robert. "All travel still difficult in D.C. area," Get There, February 9, 2010. Accessed at: http://voices.washingtonpost.com/getthere/2010/02/all_travel_still_difficult_in.html

Virginia Department of Transportation, "Crews Moving 500,000 Tons of Snow in Northern Virginia," Press release, February 7, 2010. Accessed at: http://www.virginiadot.org/newsroom/northern_virginia/2010/crews_moving_500000_tons45062.asp

Watson, Barbara McNaught; et al. "Mid Atlantic Winters," NWS Baltimore/Washington, as of 2009-10. Accessed at: http://www.erh.noaa.gov/lwx/winter/DC-Winters.htm

Weather Underground. "Daily airport history of raw METAR observations," Data for 2009-10 storms at DCA, IAD and BWI, Accessed at (and similar): http://www.wunderground.com/history/airport/KDCA/2009/12/18/DailyHistory.html

The snow shovel, an item that many Washingtonians will remember vividly when thinking back on the historic winter of 2009-10.

February 10, 2010

Kevin Ambrose

blurb.com